Welcome to Valentine's Math Fun for Kids

Get ready for a heart-filled adventure where math meets the magic of Valentine's Day!

Inside these pages, you'll find all sorts of sweet surprises:

- **Counting Puzzles**: Practice counting with hearts, flowers, and chocolates as you build your math skills.
- **Simple Math Problems**: Add up love letters, subtract candy hearts, and solve problems inspired by Valentine's Day fun.
- **Dot-to-Dot Fun**: Connect the dots to reveal adorable Valentine's symbols and scenes.
- **Word Problems**: Use your math skills to solve fun puzzles with balloons, gifts, and cupcakes.
- **Coloring Pages**: Bring your favorite Valentine's Day scenes to life with bright colors and creativity.
- **Valentine's Jokes**: Laugh along with pages of silly, heart-filled jokes that will keep you smiling through the season!

This book is perfect for little lovebugs who adore Valentine's Day and want to practice math in a fun and exciting way. Whether you're counting hearts, solving sweet puzzles, or giggling at funny jokes, there's something here for everyone.

So grab your pencil, put on your thinking cap, and let's dive into the lovely world of Valentine's math fun! Who knew learning could be this sweet?

Happy Valentine's Day and happy learning! ❤

Heart Counting Games

How Many Hearts?

1 2 3 4 5 6 7 8 9 10

 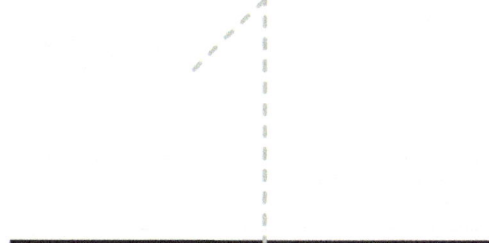

_____

_____

_____

_____

_____

How Many Cupids?

1 2 3 4 5 6 7 8 9 10

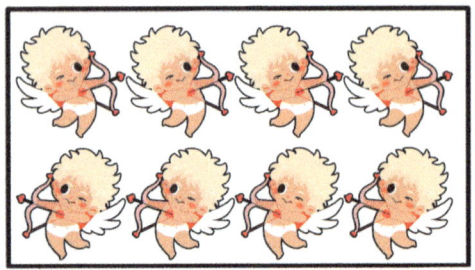

_____

_____

_____

_____

_____

How Many Chocolates?

1 2 3 4 5 6 7 8 9 10

_____

_____

_____

_____

_____

How Many Roses?

1 2 3 4 5 6 7 8 9 10

_____

_____

_____

_____

_____

How Many Candy Hearts?

1 2 3 4 5 6 7 8 9 10

_____

_____

_____

_____

_____

How Many Gifts?

1 2 3 4 5 6 7 8 9 10

_____

_____

_____

_____

_____

How Many Balloons?

1 2 3 4 5 6 7 8 9 10

_____

_____

_____

_____

_____

Match the Number to the Correct Group of Hearts

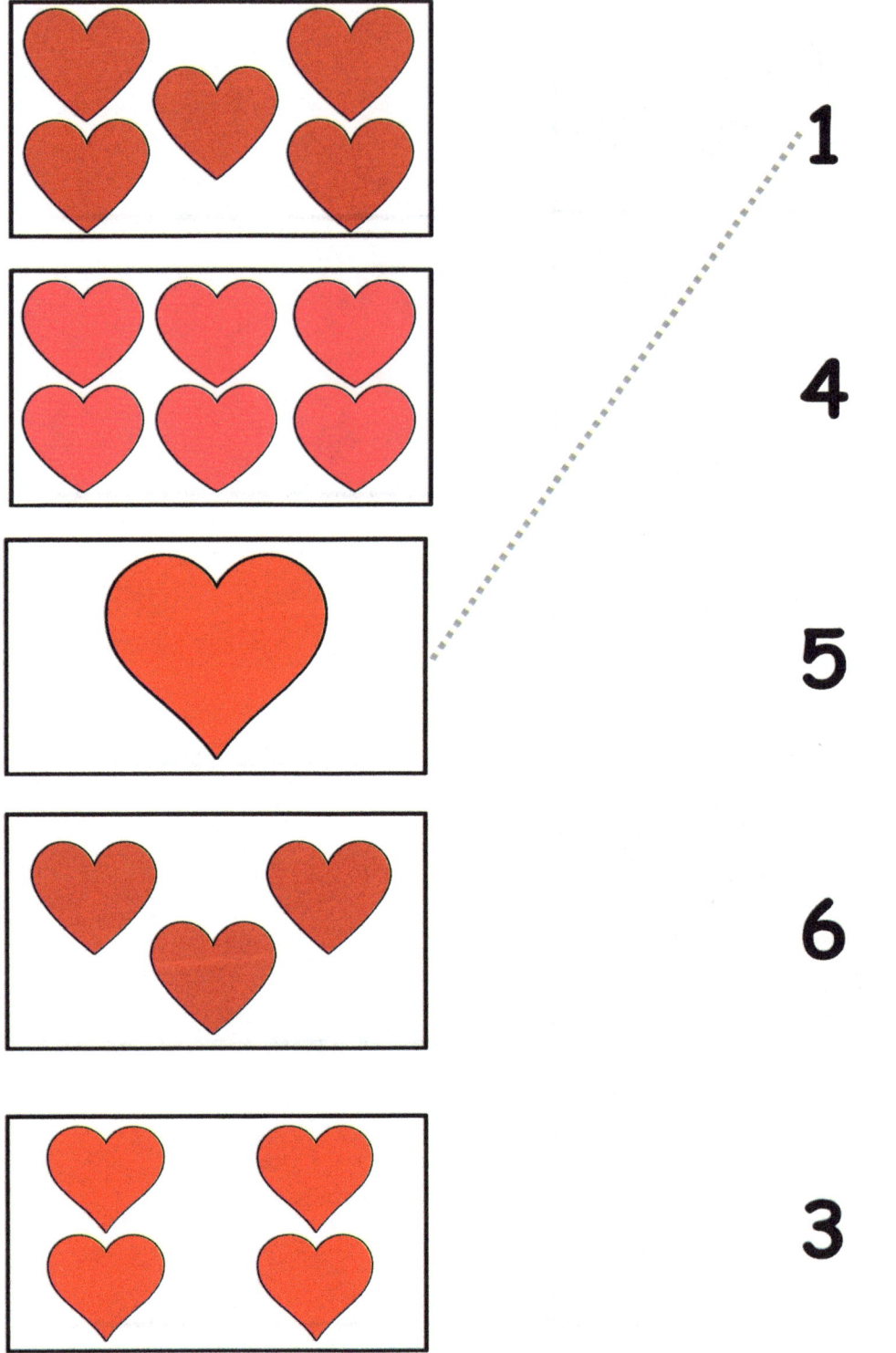

Match the Number to the Correct Group of Cupids

2

4

8

3

5

Match the Number to the Correct Group of Candy Hearts

Match the Number to the Correct Group of Gifts

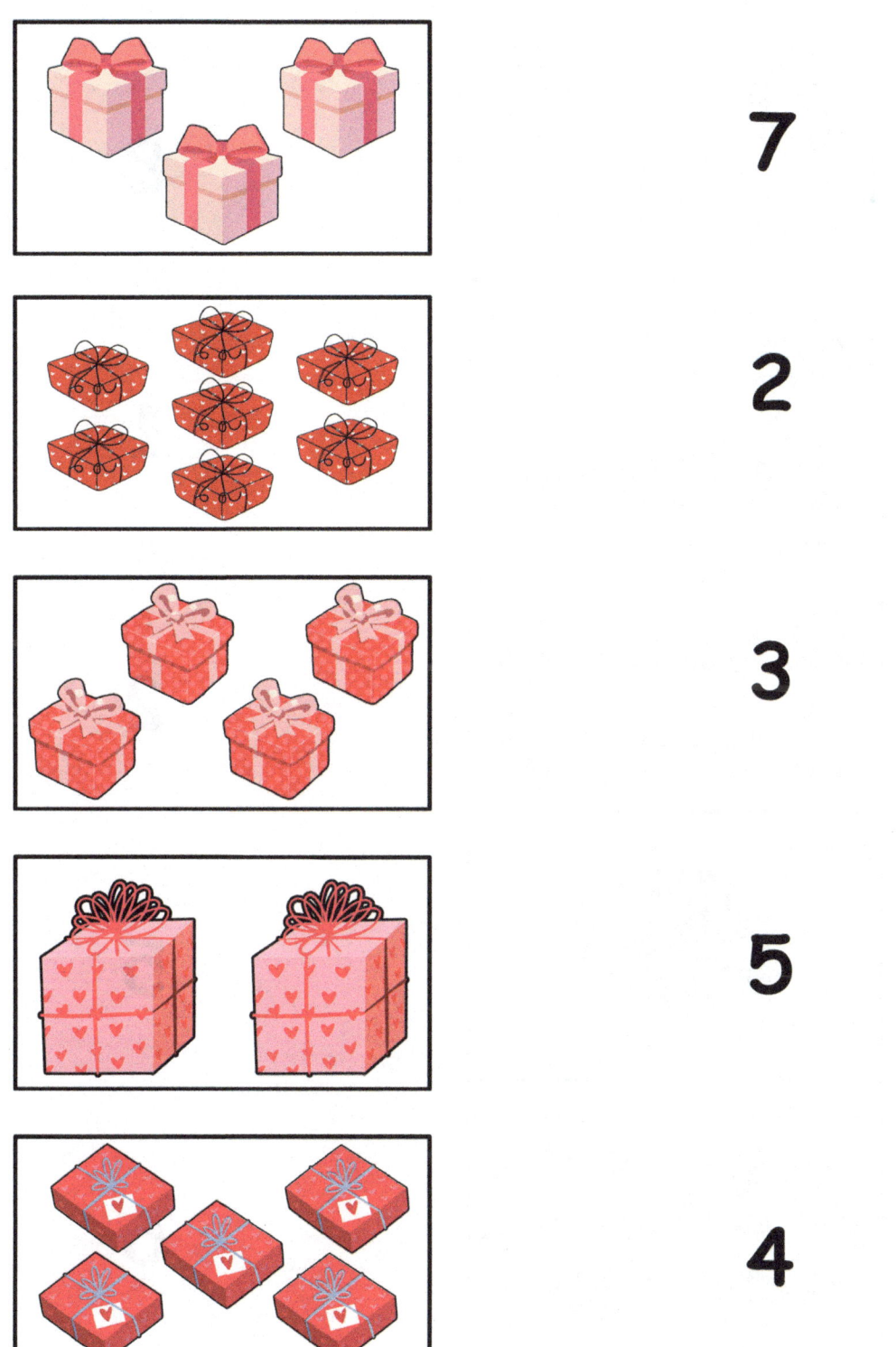

Match the Number to the Correct Group of Chocolates

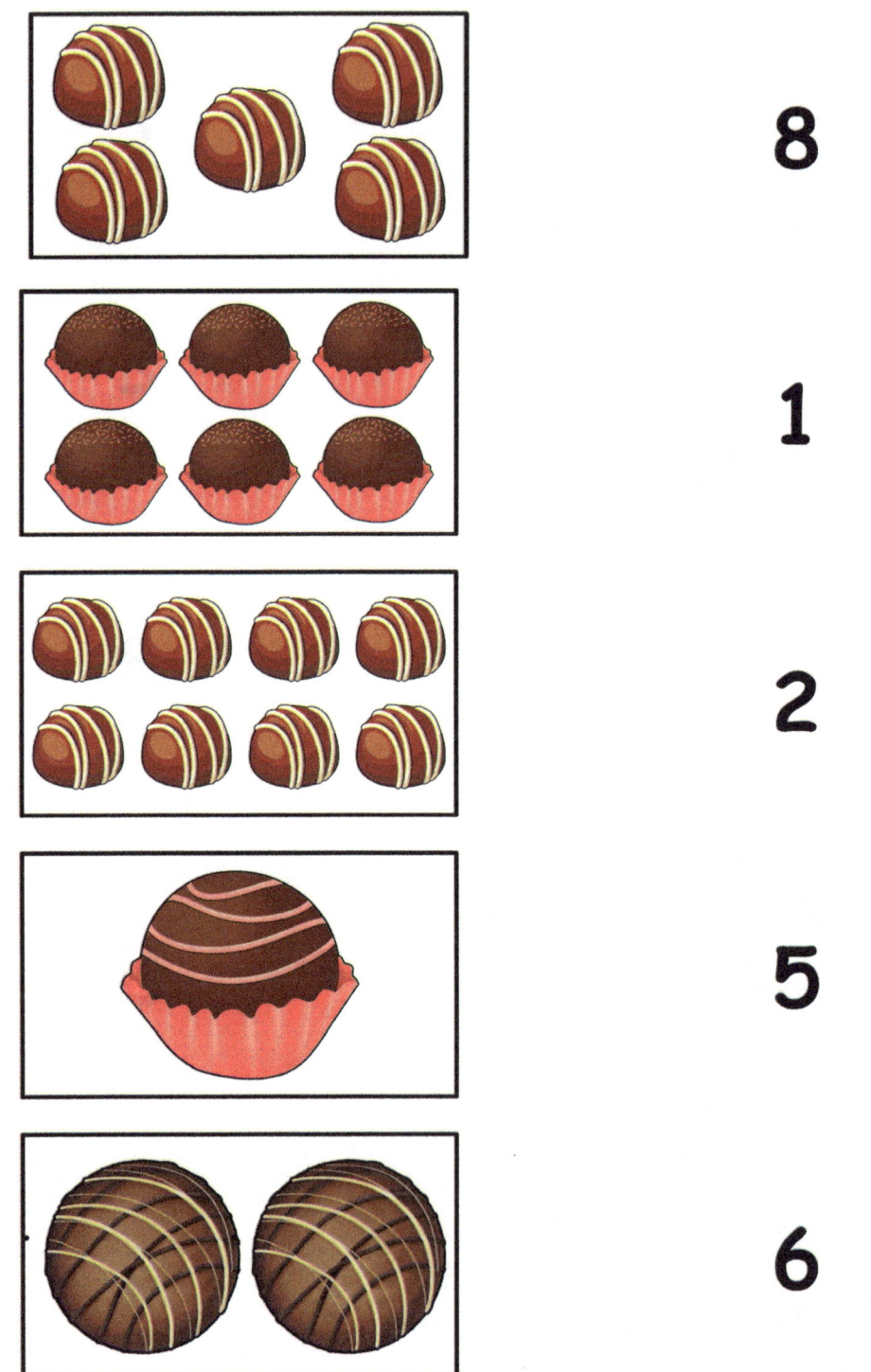

8

1

2

5

6

Match the Number to the
Correct Group of Balloons

8

1

3

5

6

Match the Number to the Correct Group of Roses

How Many of Each?

How Many of Each?

How Many of Each?

How Many of Each?

Valentine Dot-To-Dot

Connect the Dots to Send A Message Of Love

Connect the Dots to Reveal
A Tasty Treat

Connect the Dots to Unwrap The Surprise

Connect the Dots to See
Cuddly Surprise

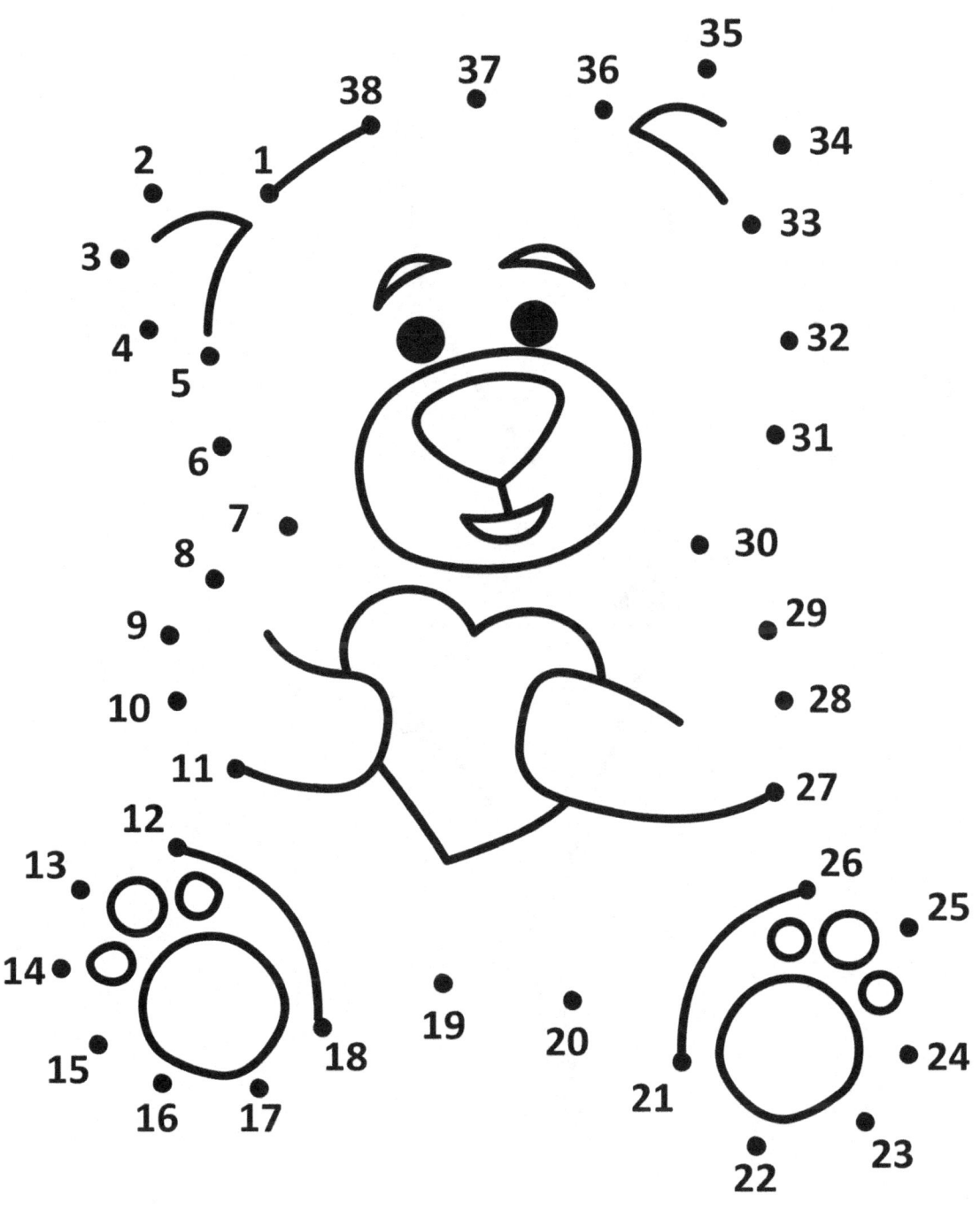

Connect the Dots to Make
Love Float

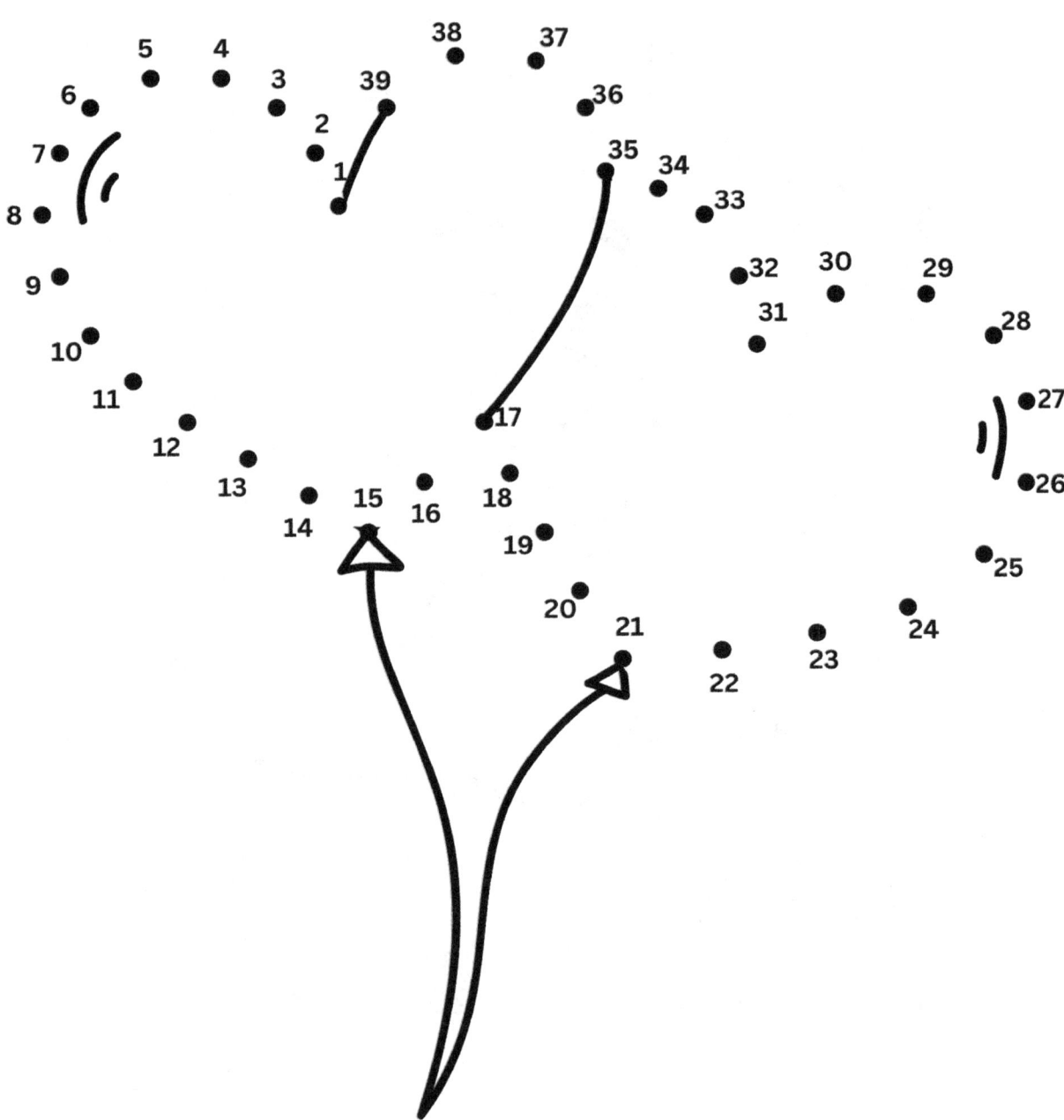

Connect the Dots to Find a Sweet Surprise

Connect the Dots to Discover
A Delicious Delight

Love
Adding and
Subtracting

Add the Chocolates

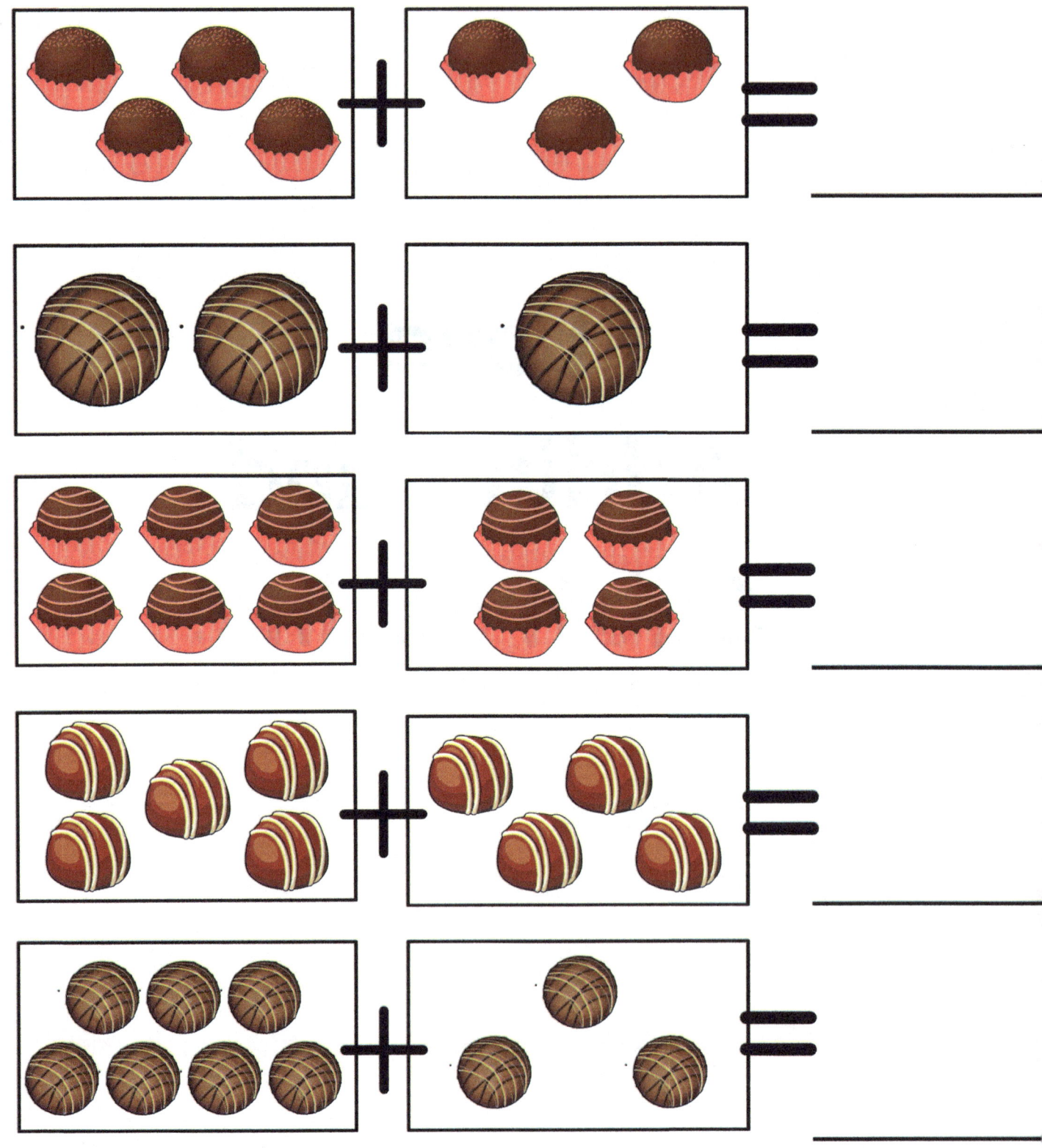

Add the Gifts

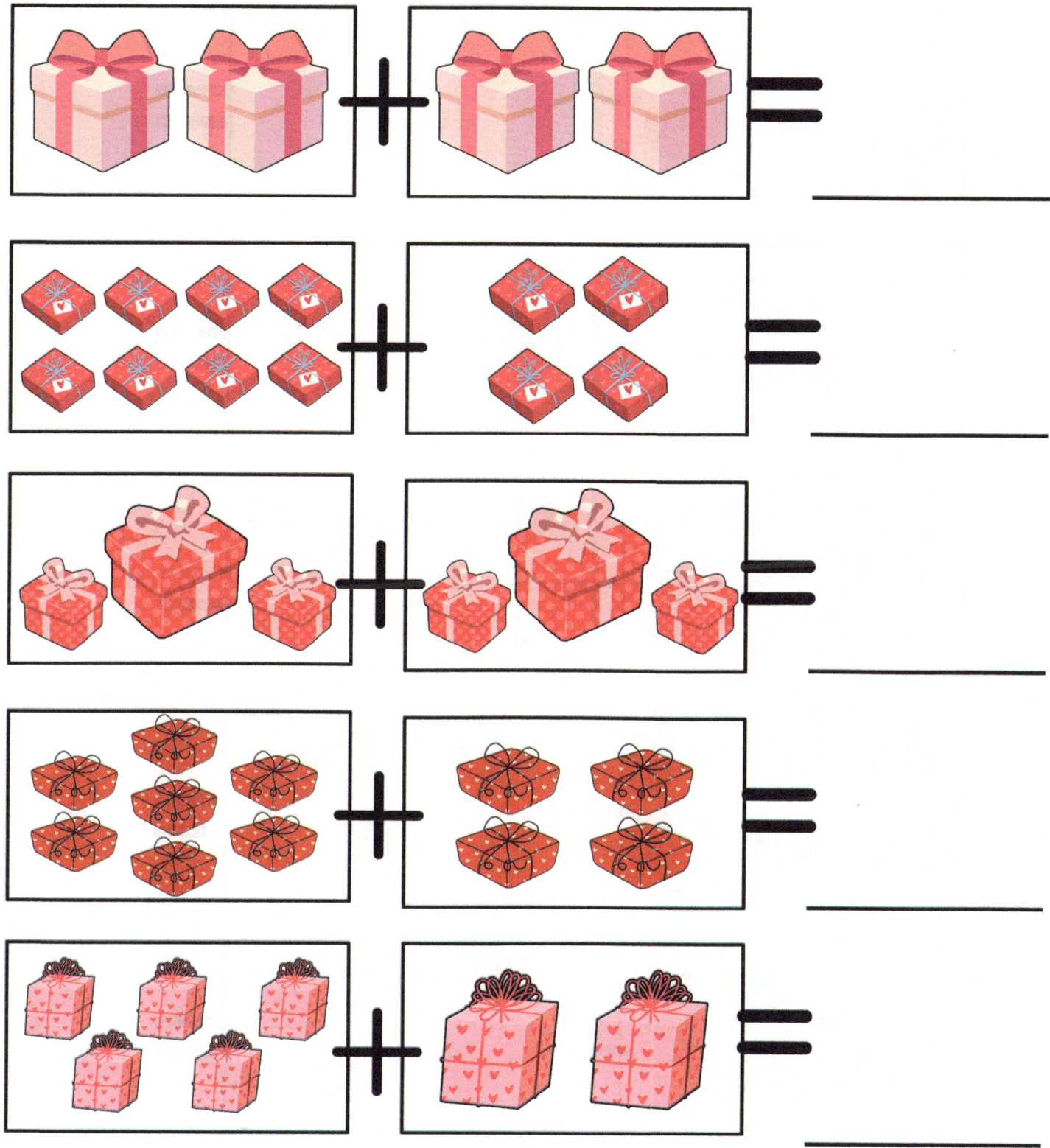

Add the Hearts

Add the Candy Hearts

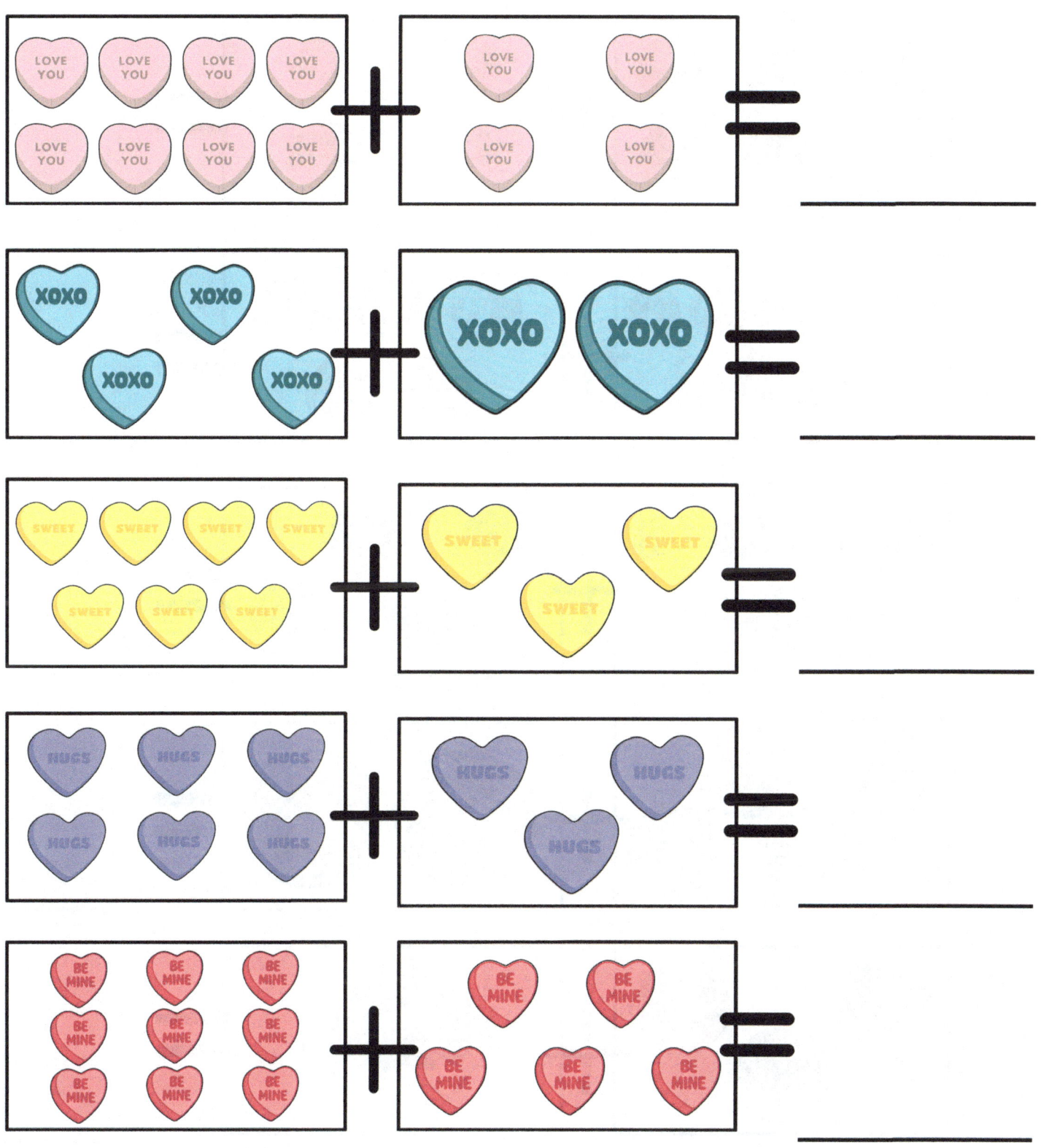

Add the Chocolates

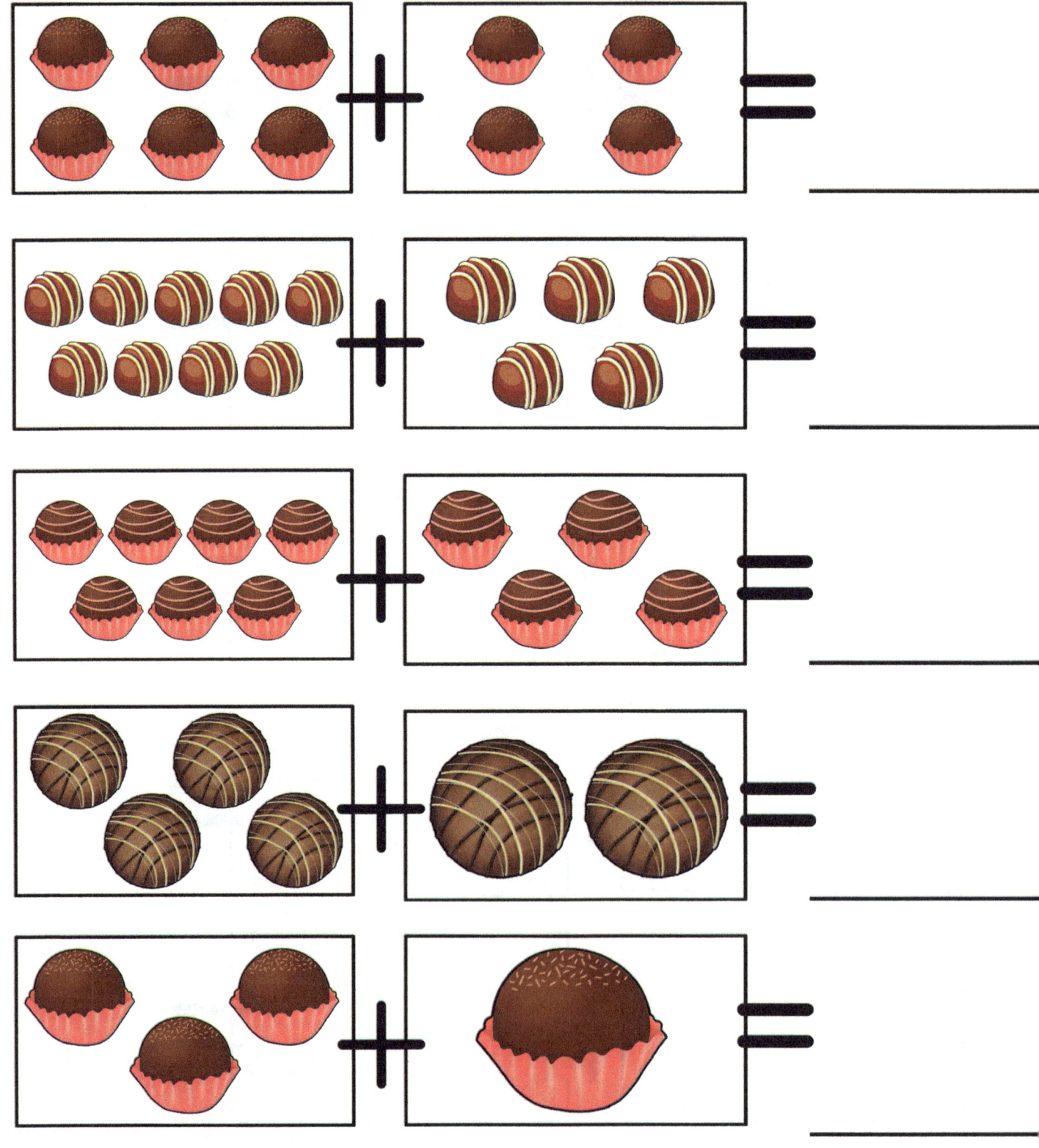

Add the Balloons

Add the Hearts

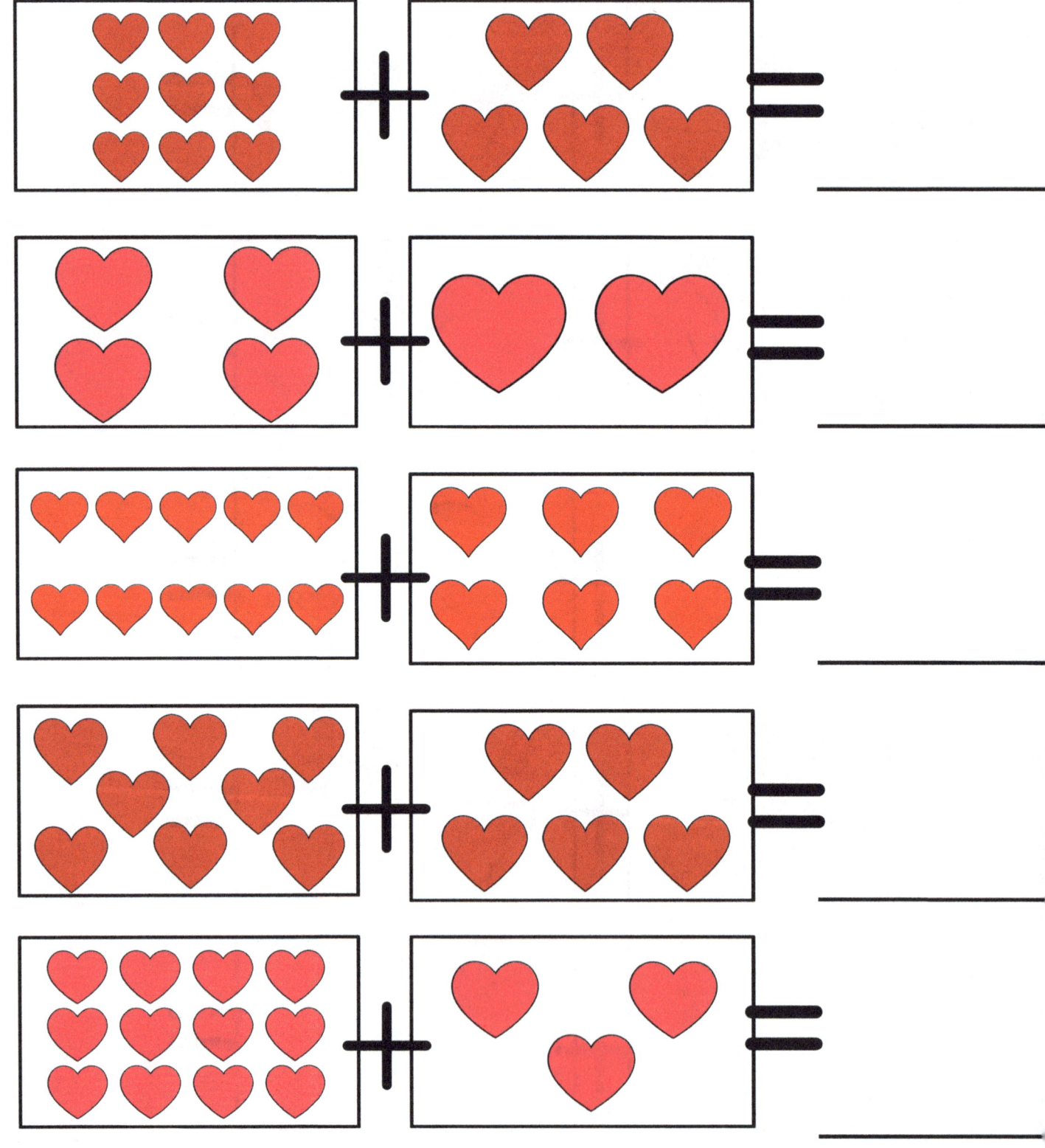

Add the Candy Hearts

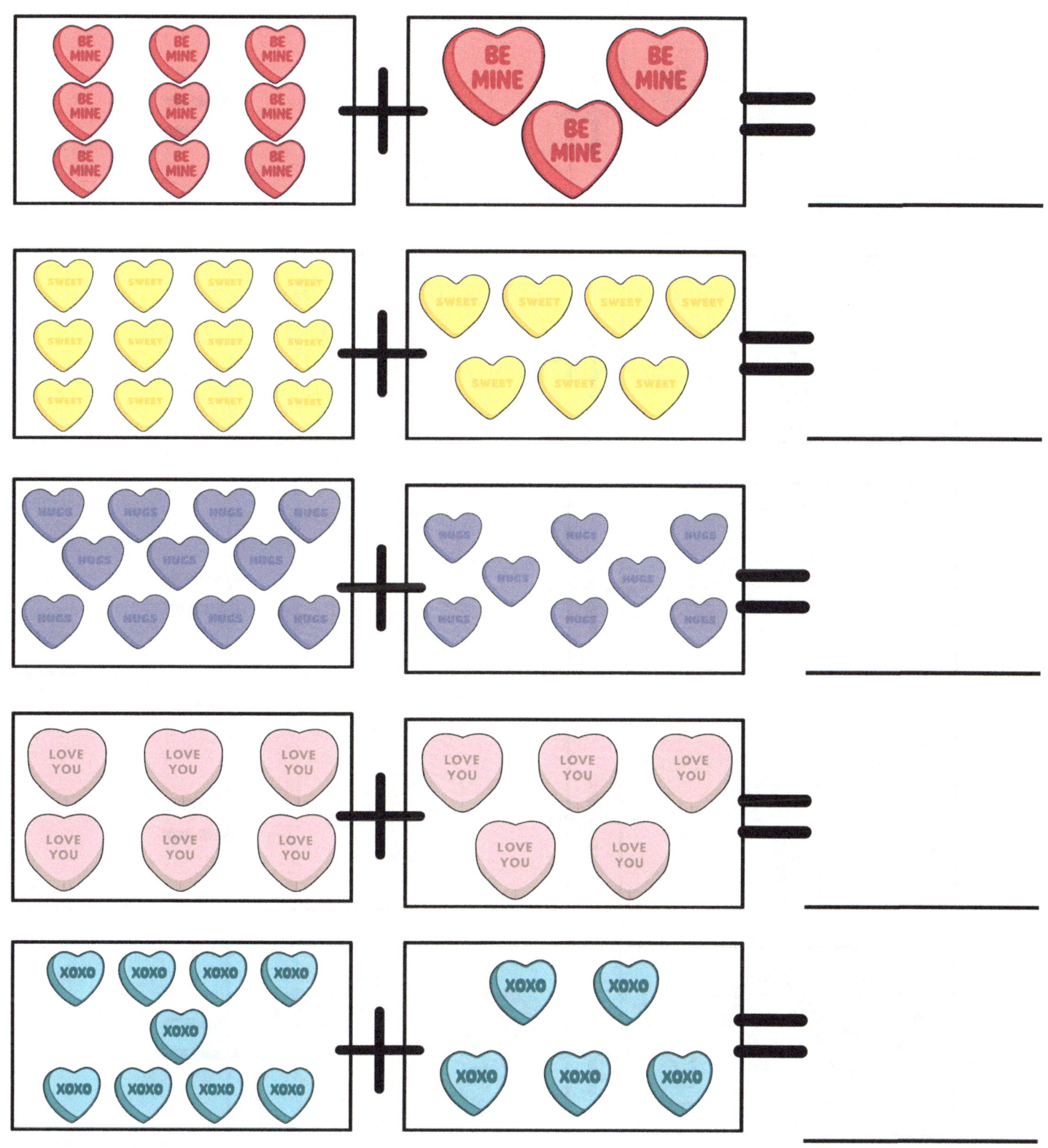

Add the Balloons

Add the Gifts

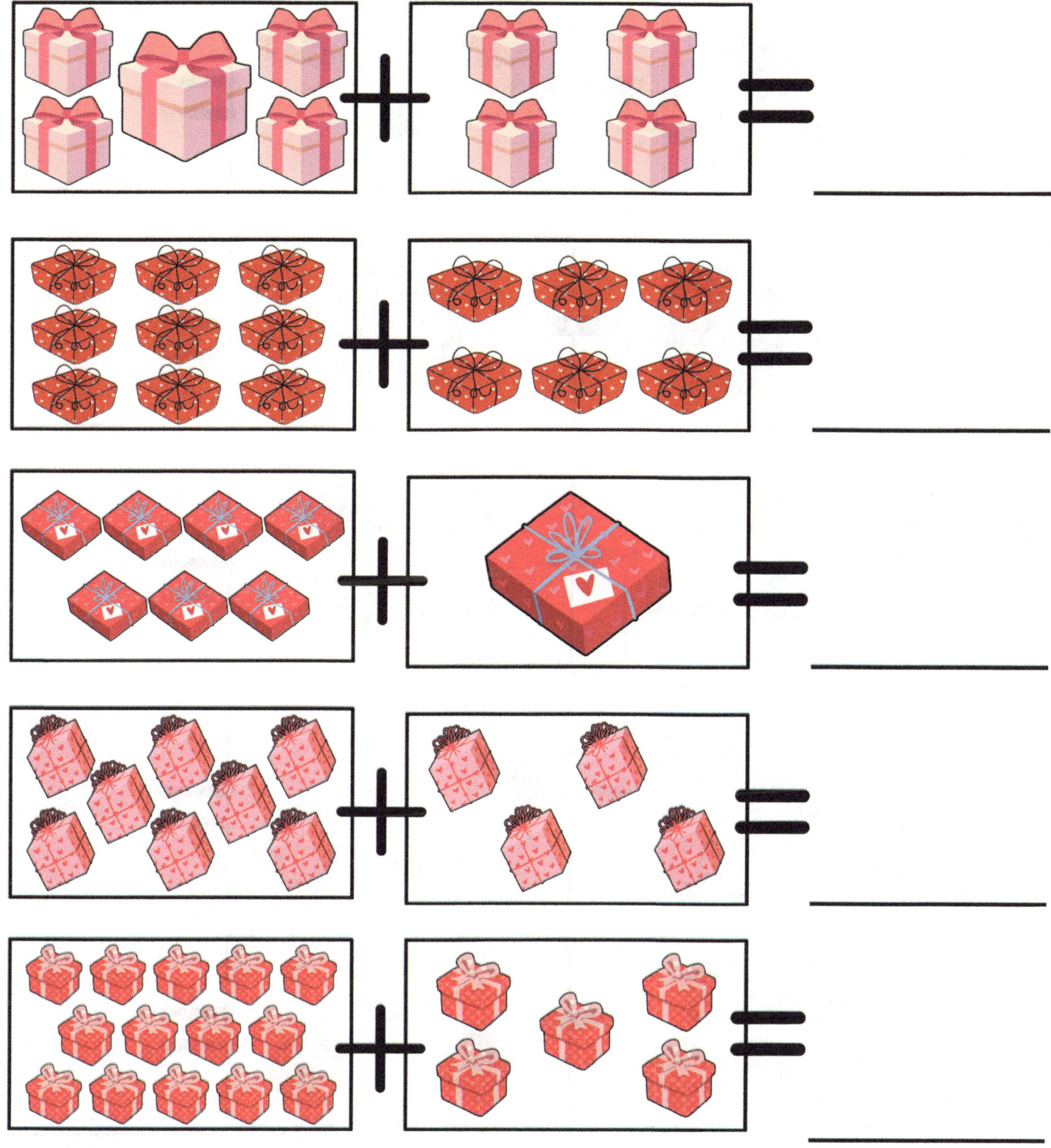

Subtract the Chocolates

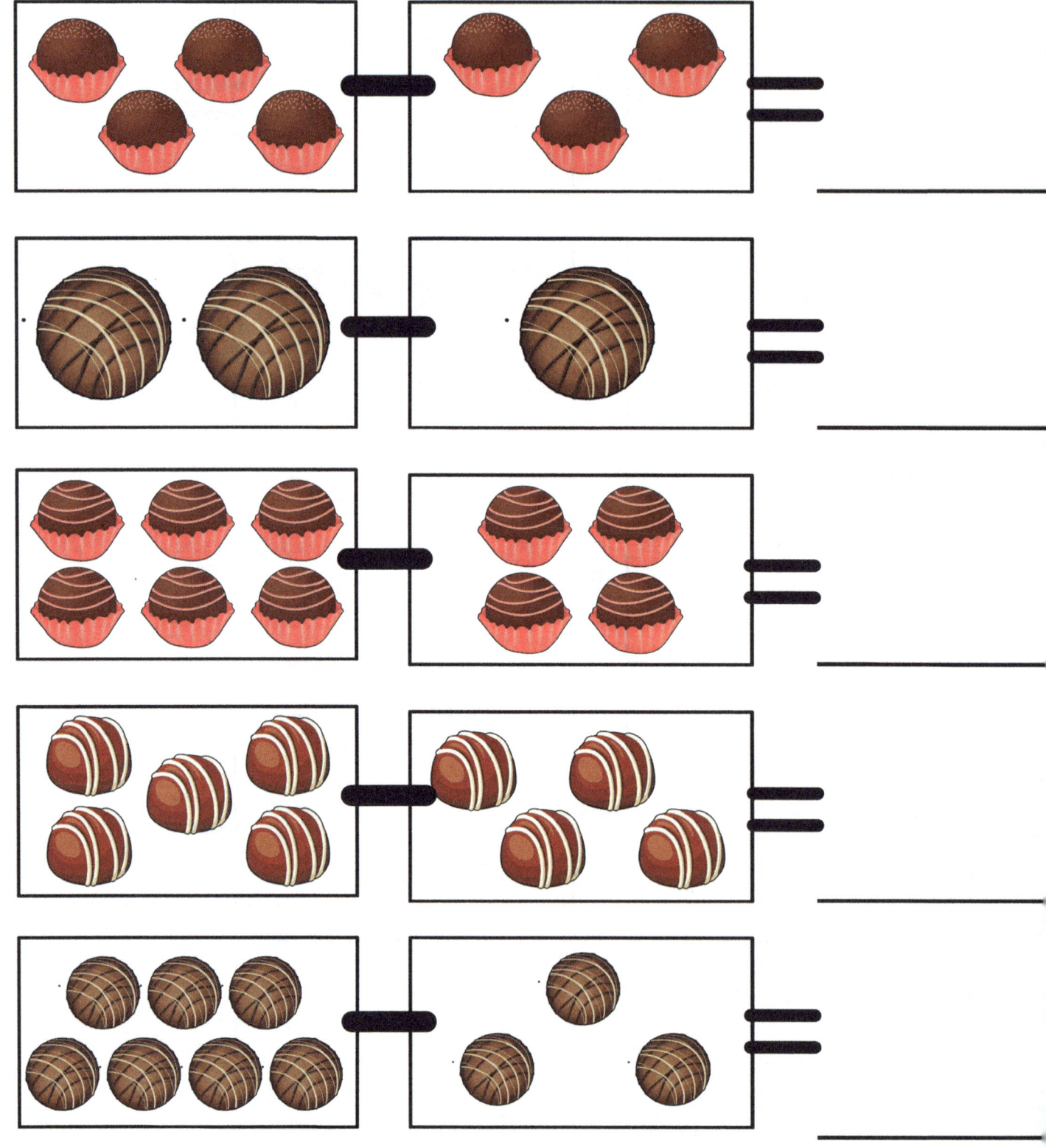

Subtract the Balloons

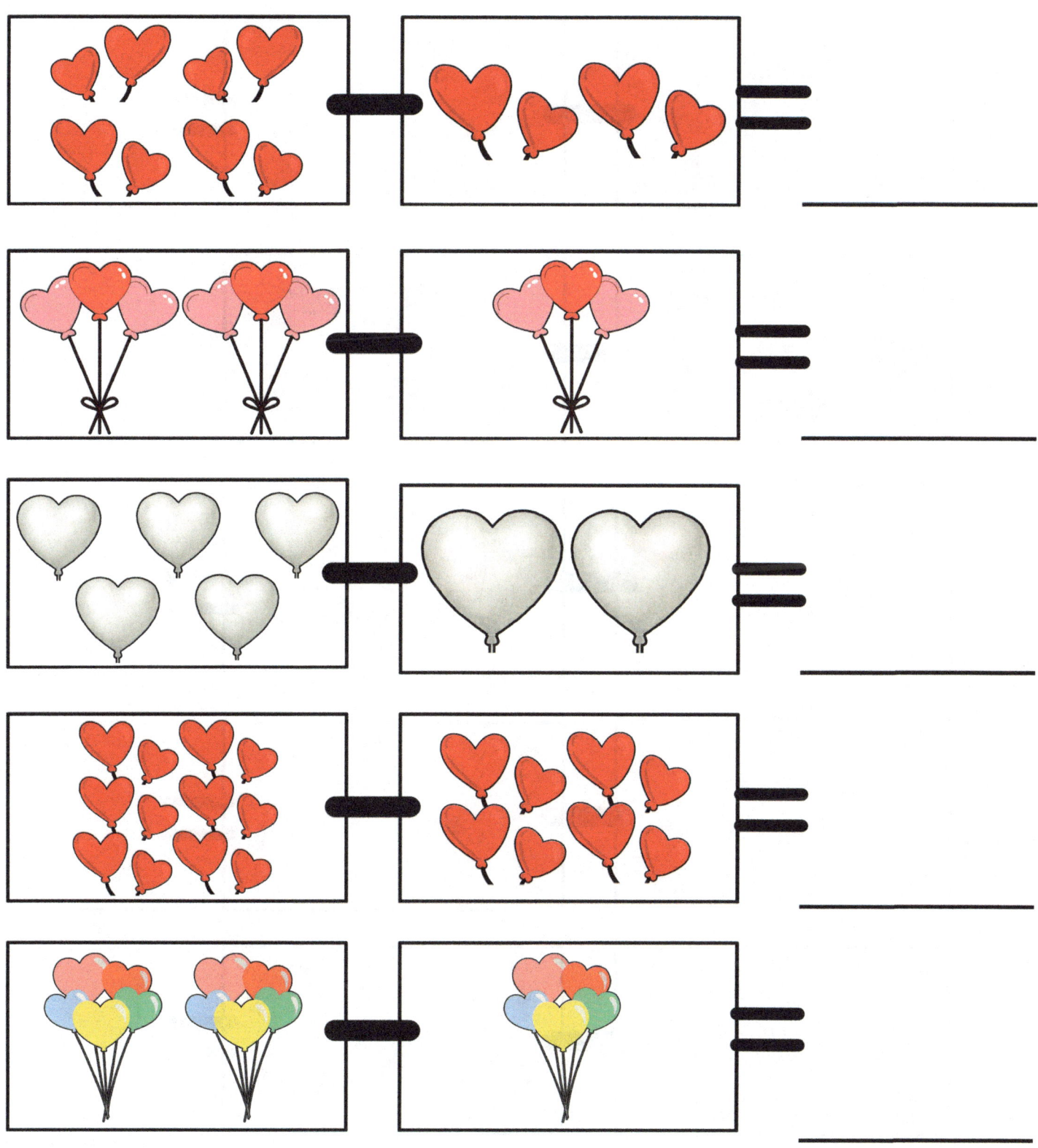

Subtract the Gifts

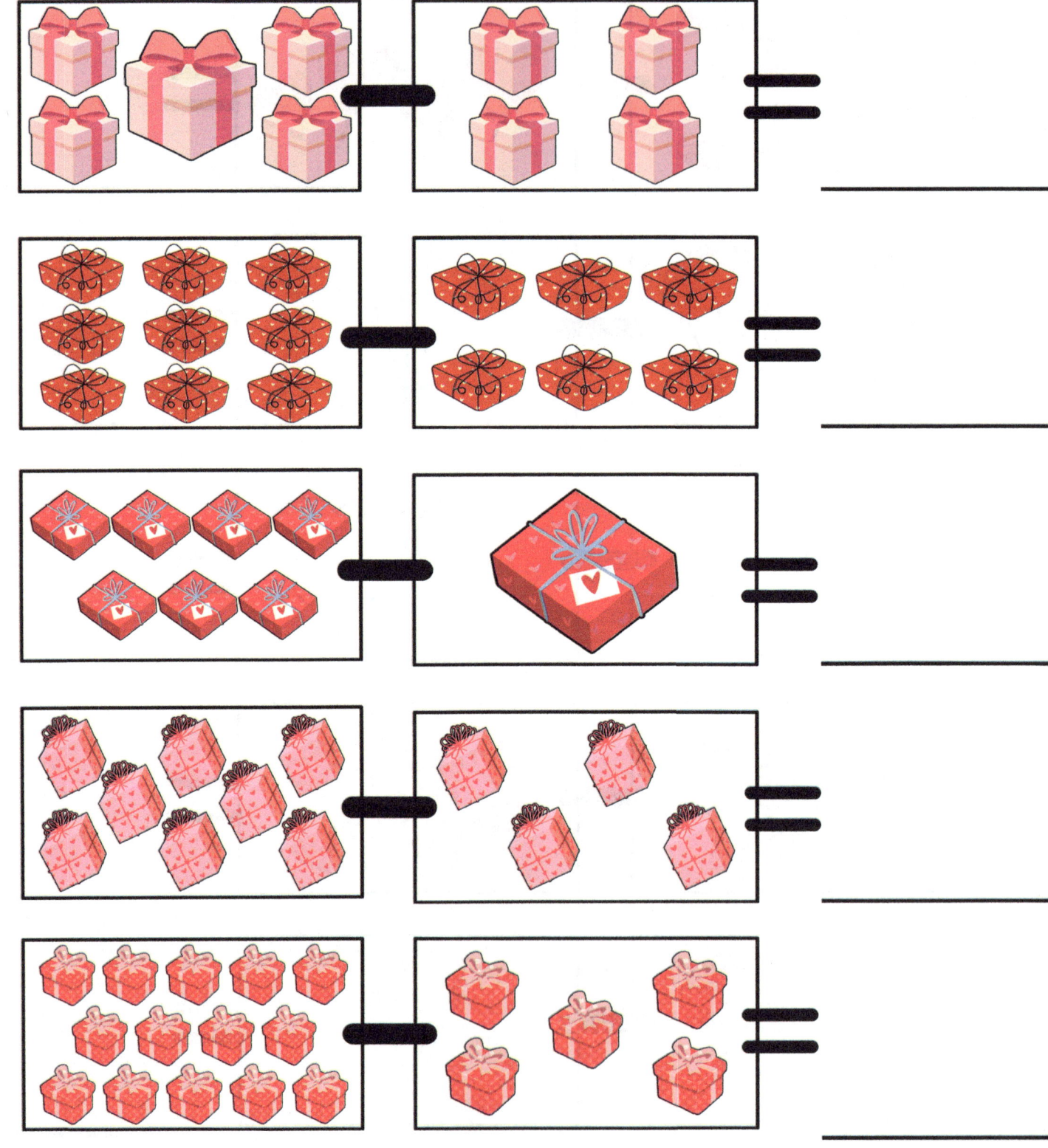

Subtract the Hearts

− = _____

− = _____

− = _____

− = _____

− = _____

Subtract the Candy Hearts

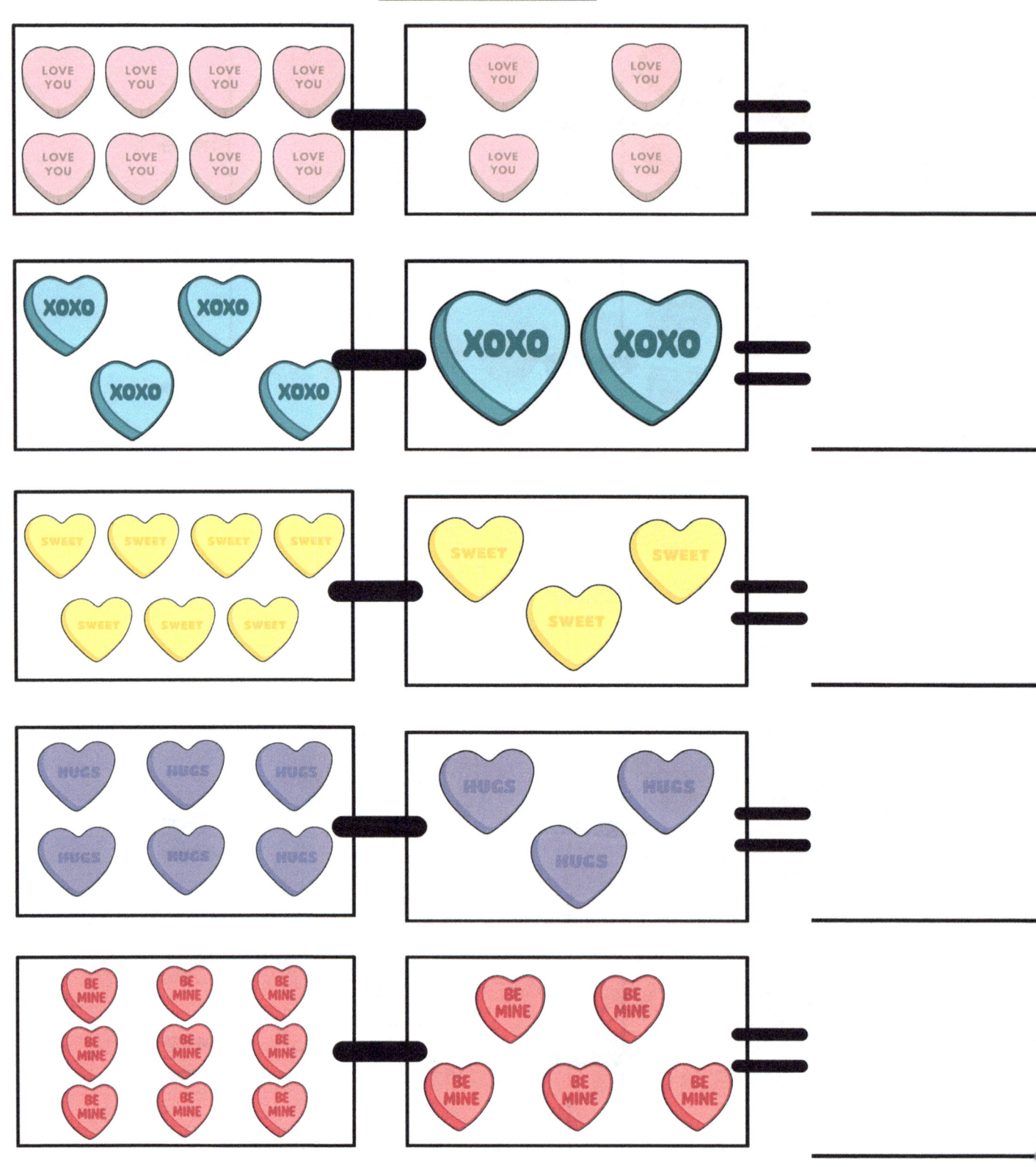

Subtract the Chocolates

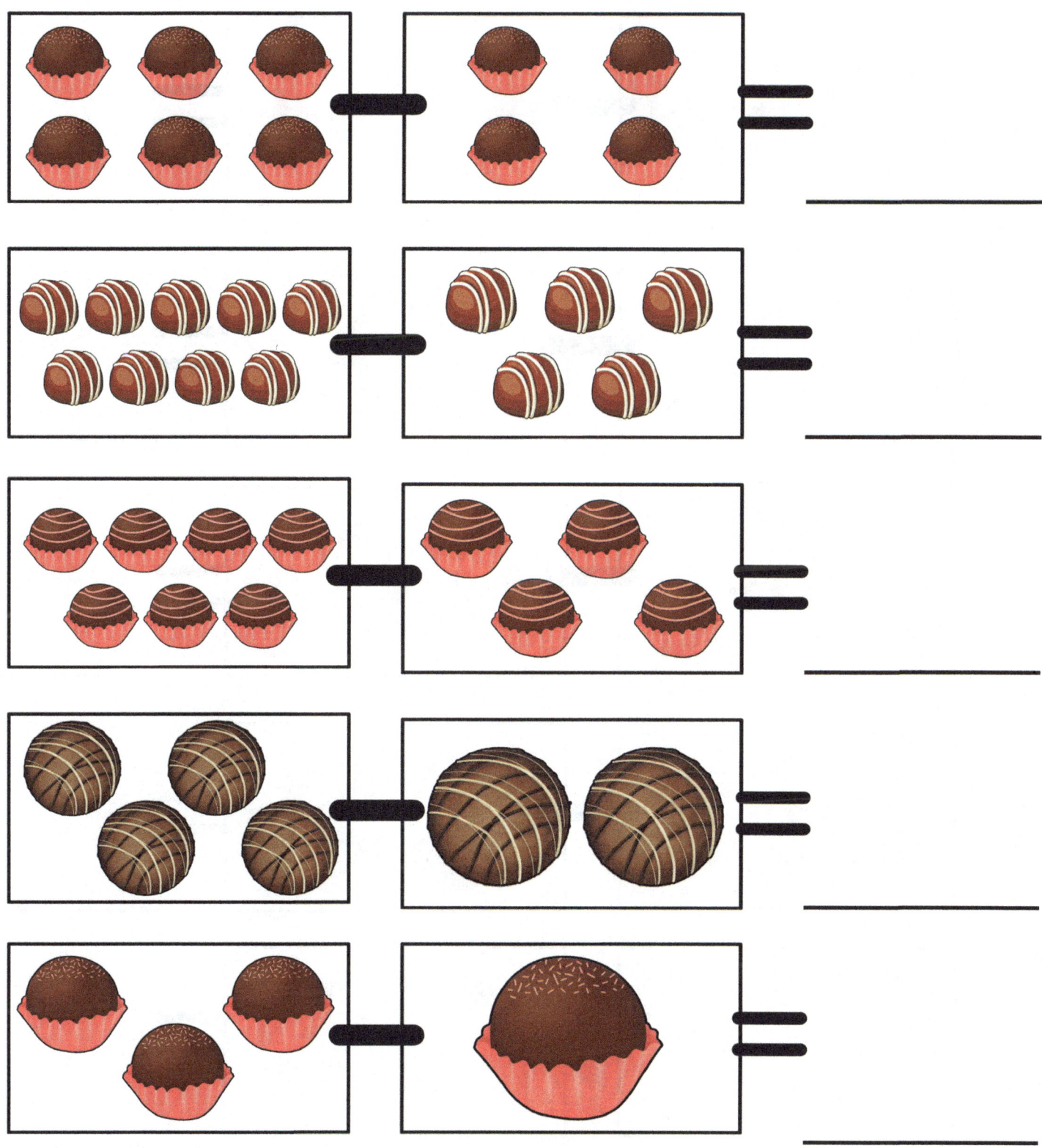

Subtract the Gifts

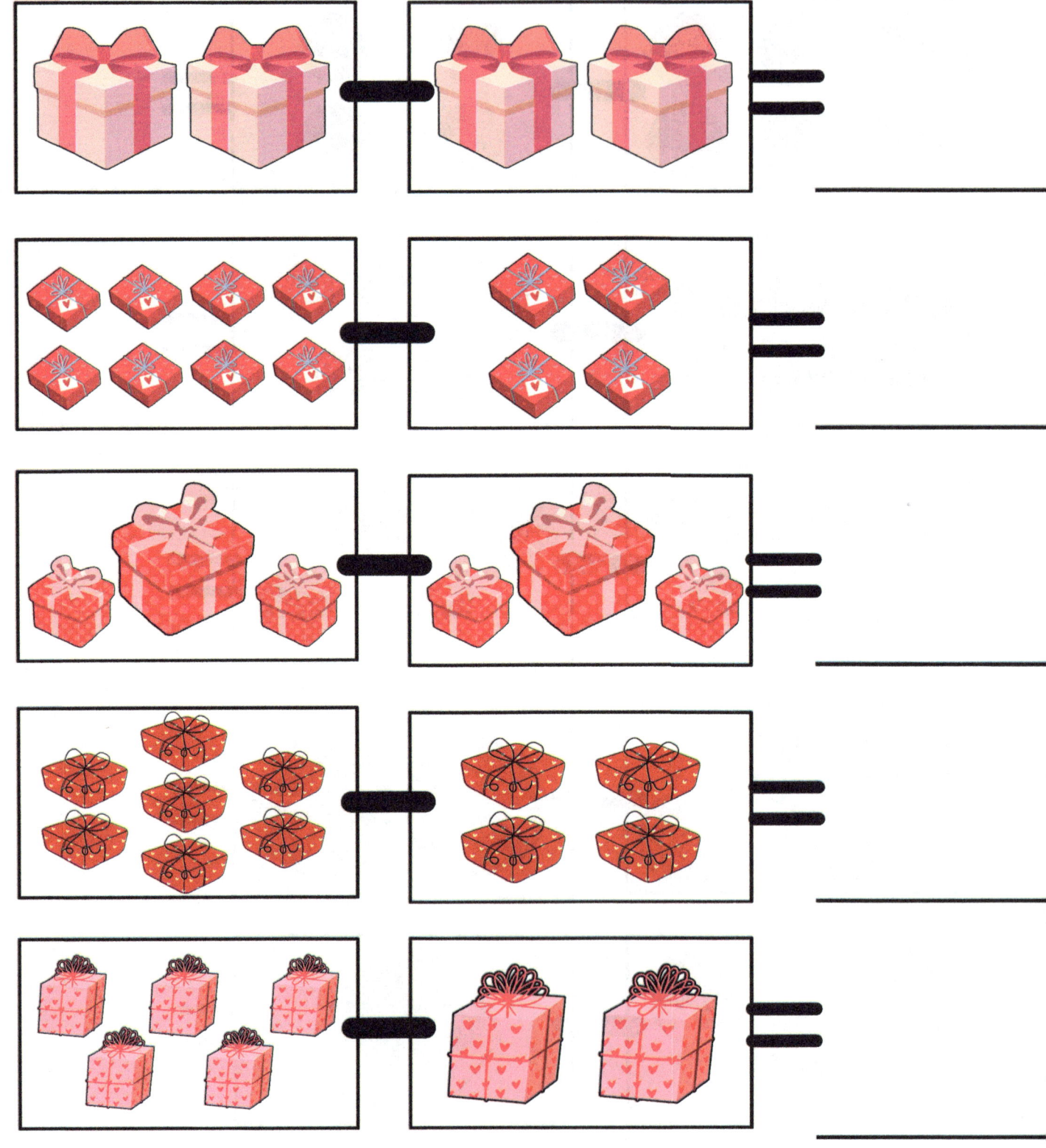

Subtract the Hearts

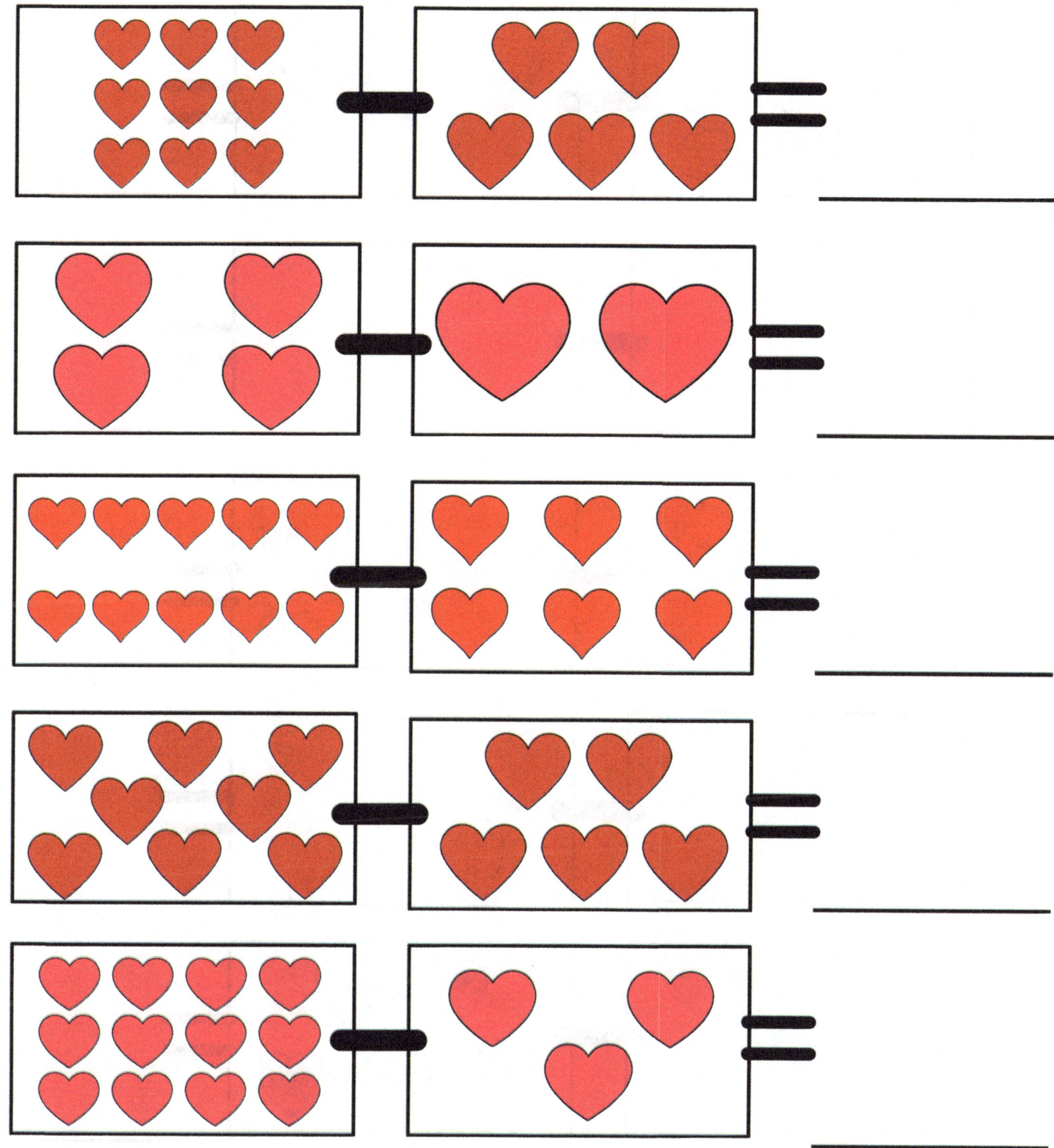

Subtract the Candy Hearts

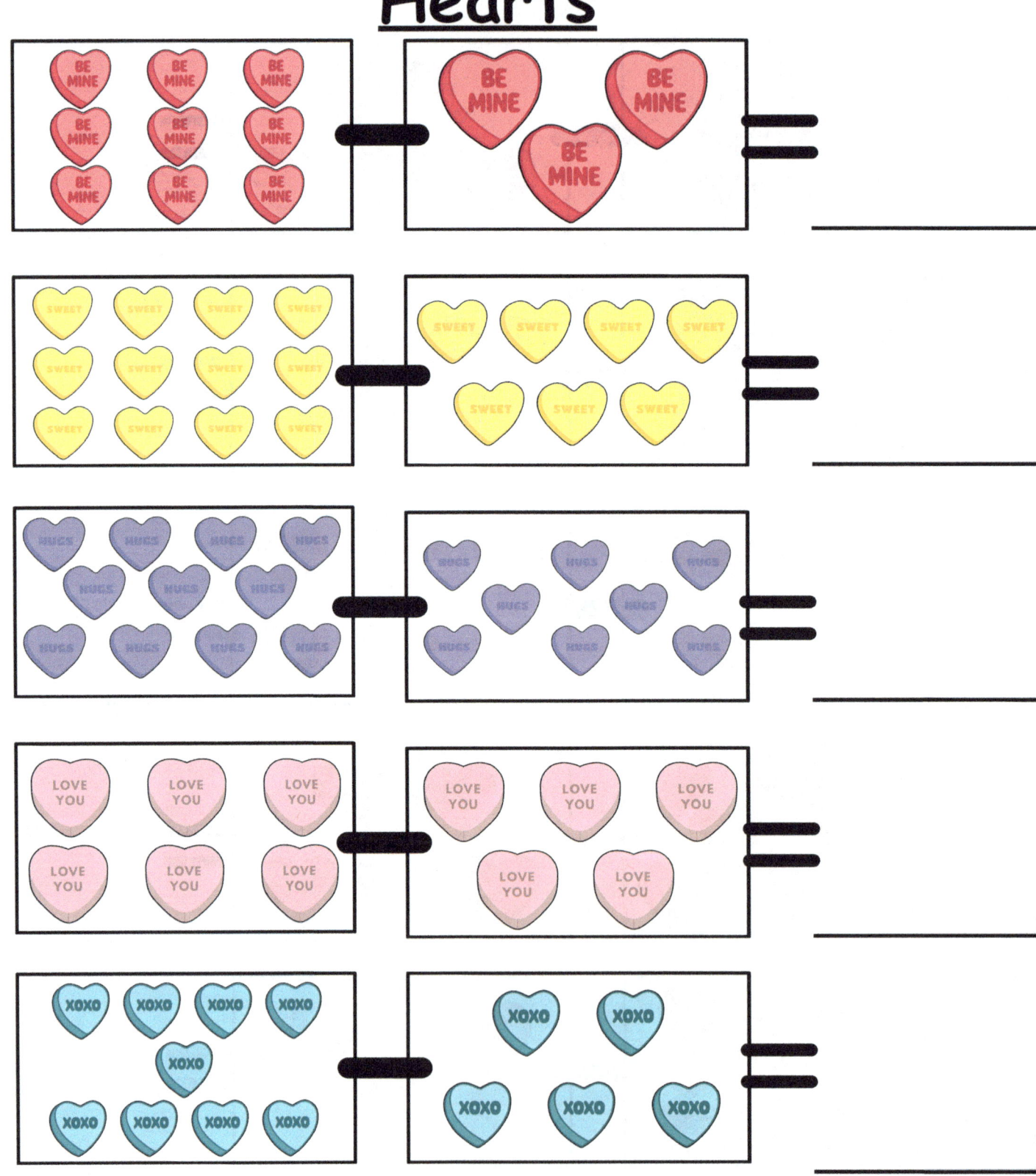

Subtract the Balloons

Love You
Patterns

Draw What Comes Next in the Pattern?

Draw What Comes Next in the Pattern?

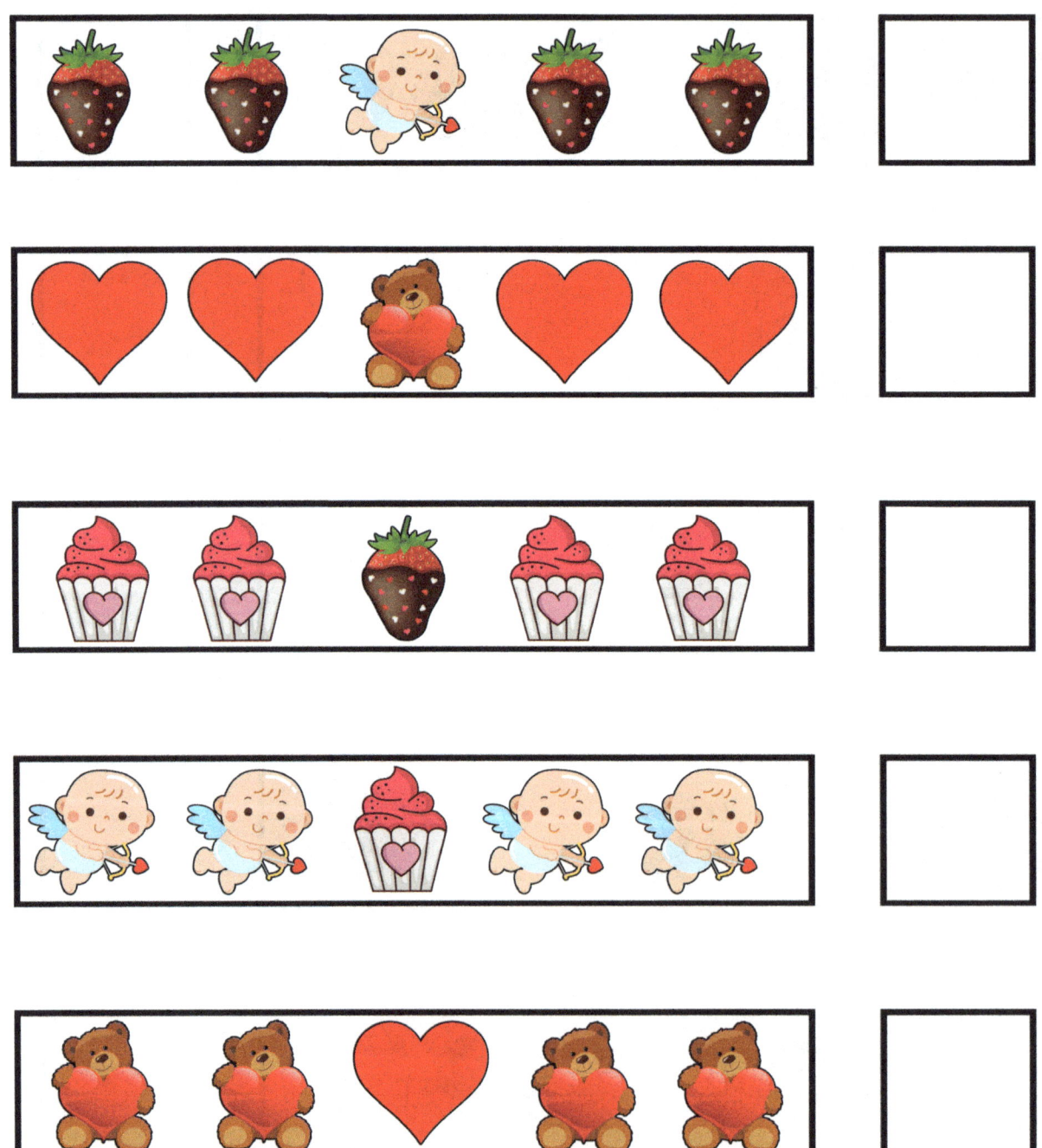

Draw What Comes Next in the Pattern?

Draw What Comes Next in the Pattern?

Draw What Comes Next in the Pattern?

Mazes
of the
Heart

Help The Cupid Get To The Love Letter

Help The Teddy Bear Find The Hearts

Help The Box Of Chocolates Find the Gift Bag

Help The Balloons Float To The Clouds

Help The Puppy Find
Its Valentine's Gift

Help The Cat Find Its Valentine's Gift

Help The Bouquet Of Flowers Reach The Doorstep

Help The Porcupine Find Its Valentine's Surprise

Help the Gift Reach the Gift Table

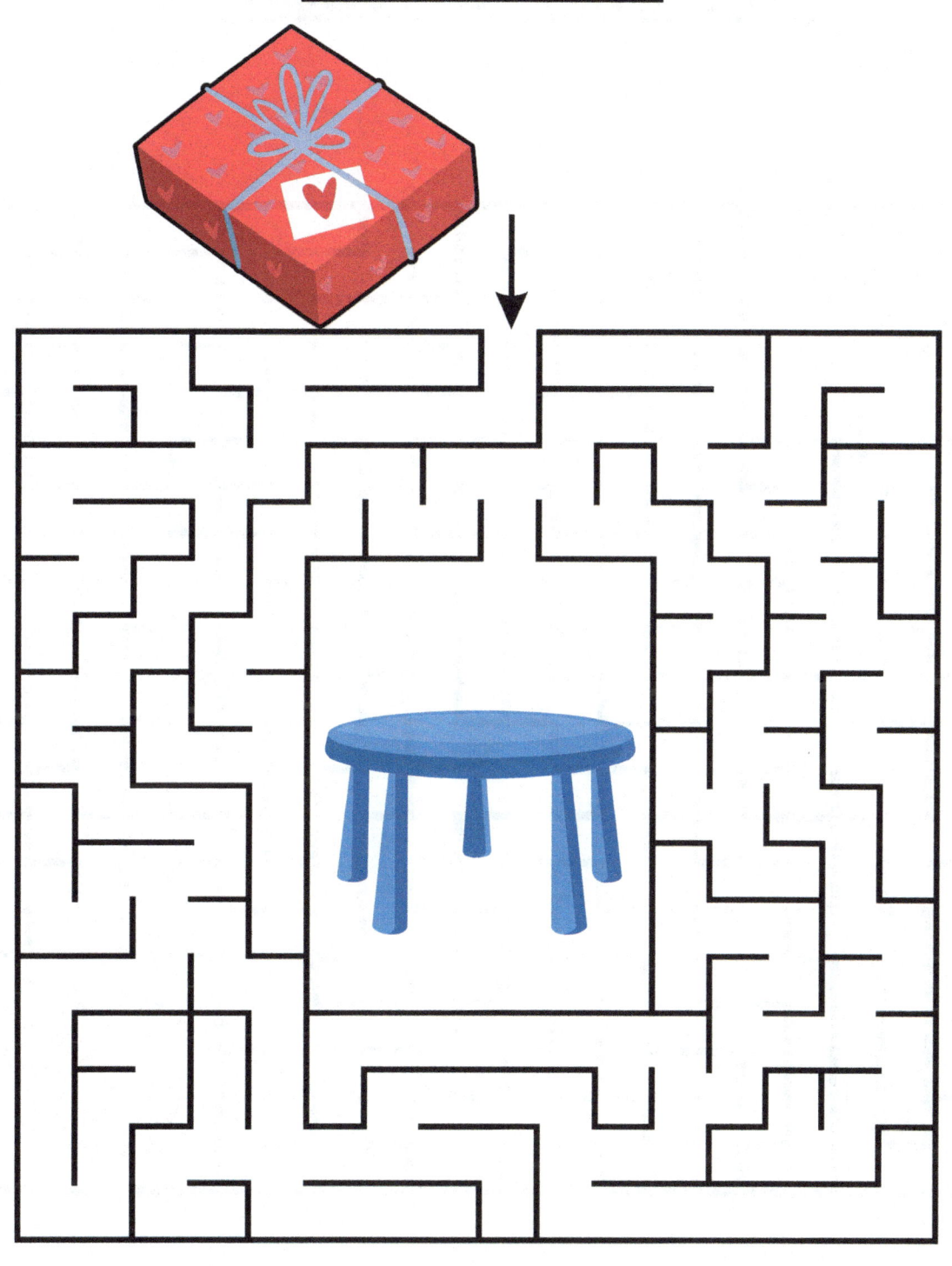

Help the Cookie get to the Hot Chocolate

Fill In the Missing Numbers to Help The Envelope Reach The Mailbox

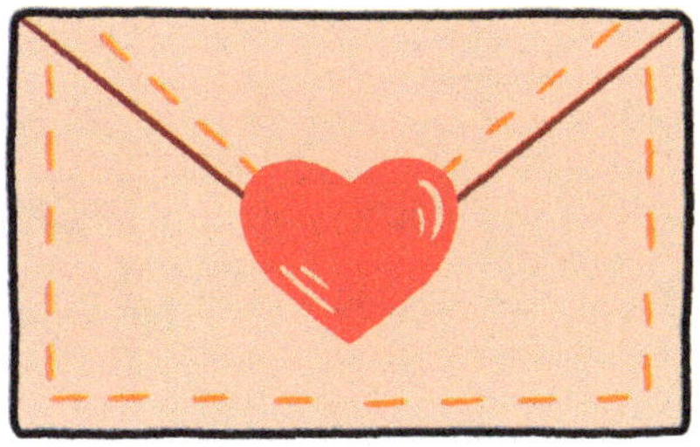

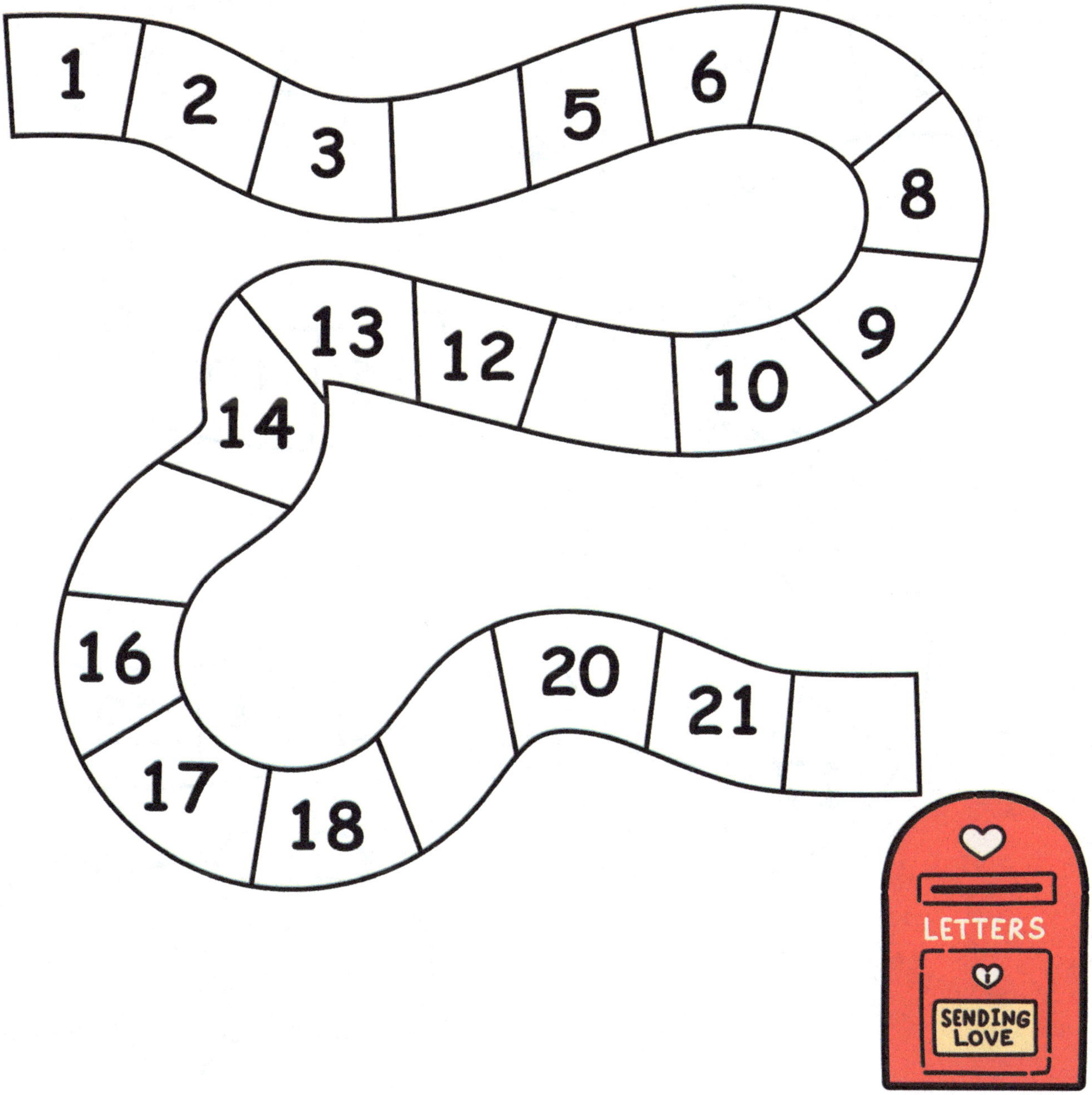

1 2 3 __ 5 6 __ 8 9 10 __ 12 13 14 __ 16 17 18 __ 20 21 __

Fill In The Missing Numbers to Help the Heart Balloons Float To The Sky

Fill In The Missing Numbers to Help the Bear Deliver The Chocolates

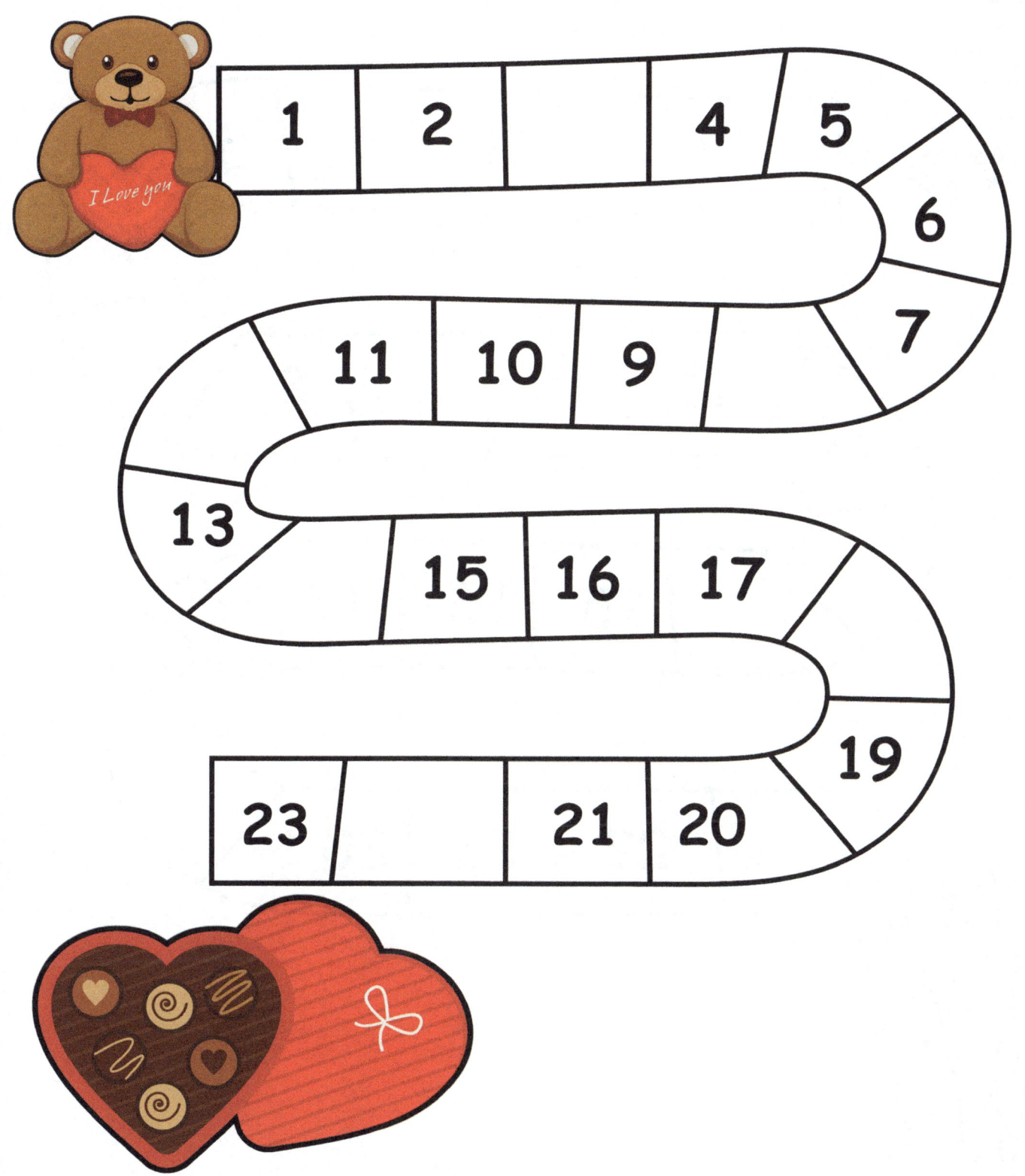

Fill In The Missing Numbers to Help the Bee Find The Flower Garden Of Love

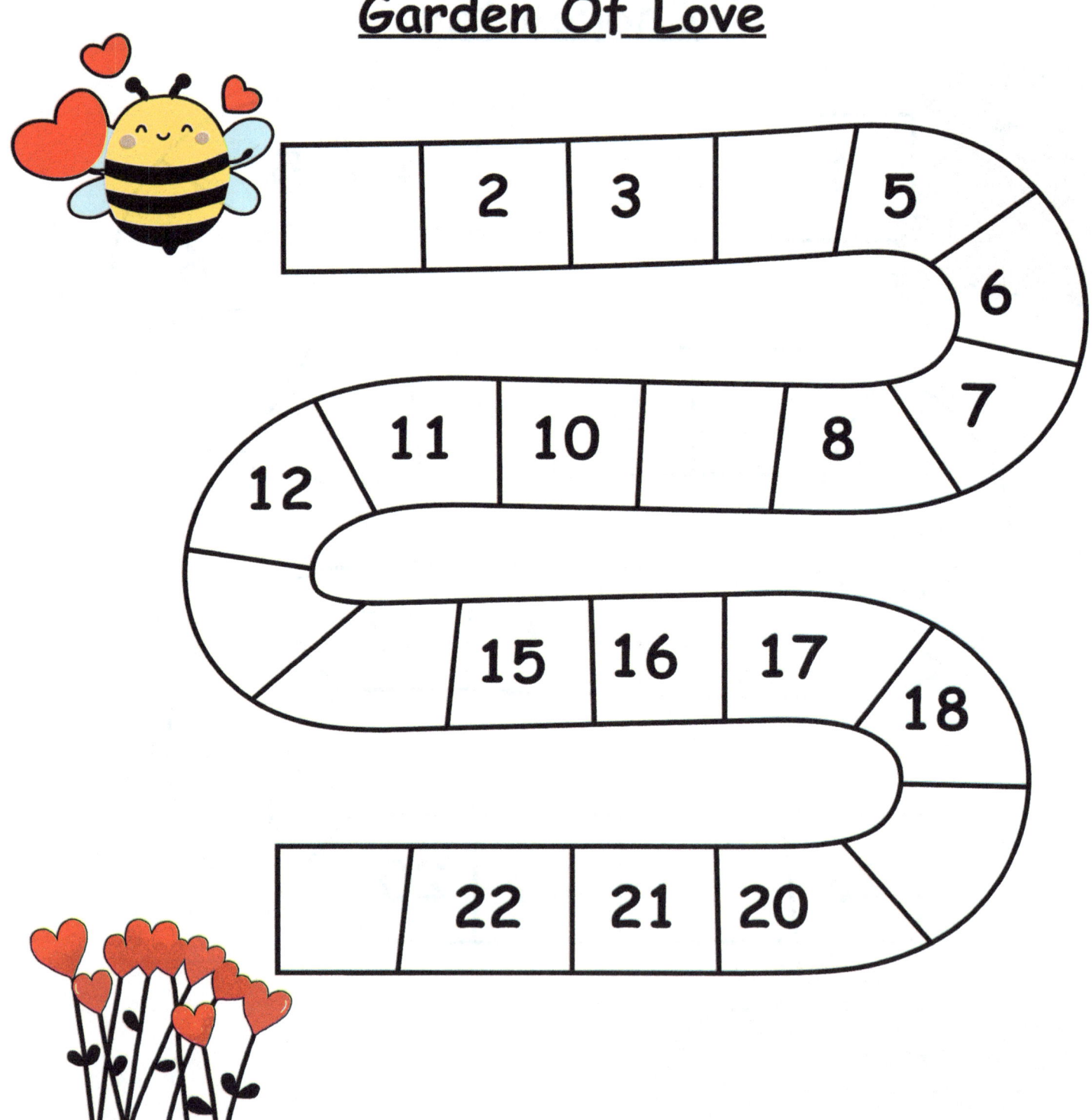

Fill In The Missing Numbers to Help the Chocolate Get To The Box

Fill In The Missing Numbers to Help the Chocolate Strawberry Get to the Plate

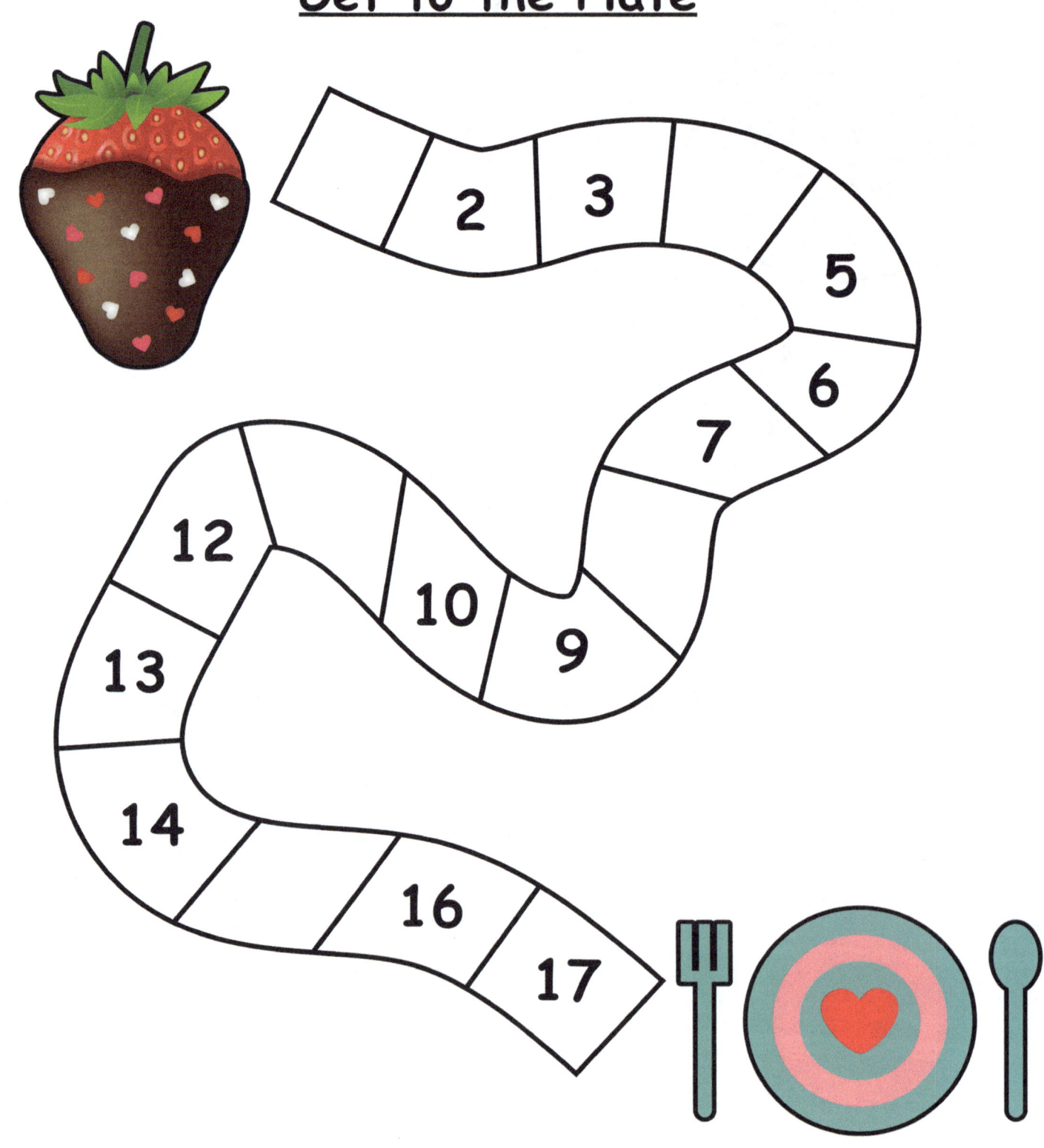

Fill In The Missing Numbers to Help the Teddy Bear Get to the Gift Box

Fill In The Missing Numbers to Help the Cookie Get to the Oven

Fill In The Missing Numbers to Help the Bunny Find The Carrot

Fill In The Missing Numbers to Help the Present get to the Gift Table

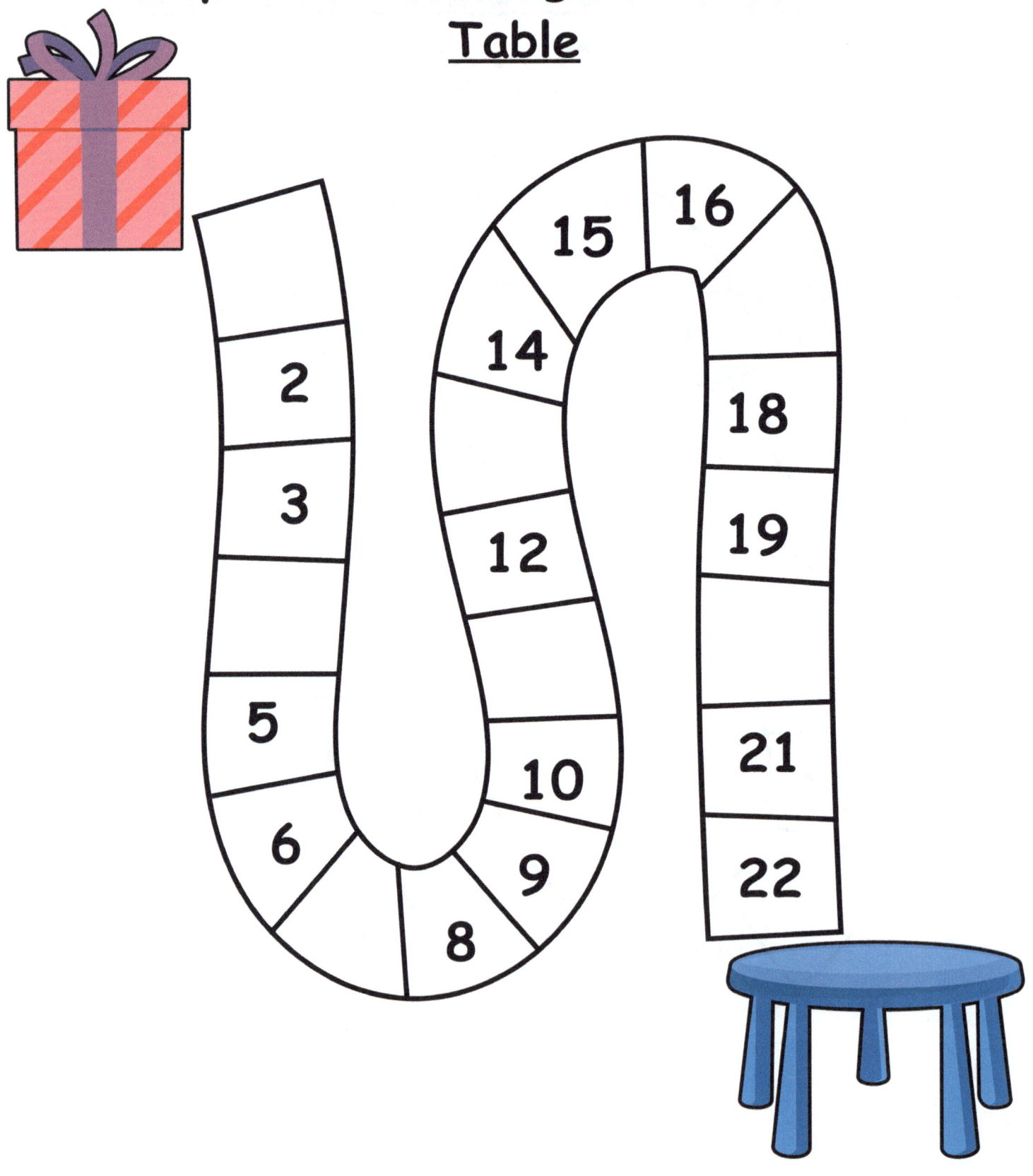

Fill In The Missing Numbers to Help Love Bug Find Its Mate

Fill In The Missing Numbers to Help Alligator Find Its Friend

Lovely
Math
Mysteries

Cupid shot 3 arrows at hearts and then 2 more arrows. How many arrows did Cupid shoot?

Emma got 4 Valentine's cards at school then got 3 more from her neighbors. How many cards does Emma have now?

Tom had 2 candy hearts and got 2 more from his mom. How many candy hearts does Tom have?

A bear is holding 5 balloons, and 1 balloon floats away. How many balloons are left?

Sarah baked 3 cupcakes and her dad baked 2 more. How many cupcakes do they have?

There are 16 candies in the box. If 4 are taken, how many are still in the box?

Luke made 3 red hearts and 4 pink hearts. How many hearts did Jack make?

There are 7 flowers in a bouquet. If 3 flowers fall out, how many are still in the bouquet?

There are 9 cookies on a plate. If 3 are eaten, how many cookies are left?

Mia is holding 6 heart balloons, and her brother gives her 2 more. How many heart balloons does Mia have now?

Lilly gave 5 Valentine's cards to her classmates and 1 to her teacher. How many cards did she give out?

Jonah bakes 2 batches of cookies, and each batch has 6 cookies. How many cookies are there in total?

A bunny picked 4 red flowers and 3 yellow flowers. How many flowers does the bunny have?

Uncle Jacob brings 6 gifts and gives 2 away. How many gifts are left?

A cupcake has 6 red sprinkles and 2 pink sprinkles. How many sprinkles are on the cupcake?

A box has 6 chocolates inside, and someone adds 4 more. How many chocolates are in the box now?

A lovebird has 5 seeds and gives 2 to its friend. How many seeds does the lovebird have now?

Your cousin has 8 cookies in a jar. If he eats 5, how many cookies are left for you?

In a garden, there are 4 pink flowers, 4 yellow flowers, and 3 red flowers. How many flowers are in the garden?

If Sarah has 1 pair of mittens and gets 1 more pair, how many mittens does she have in total?

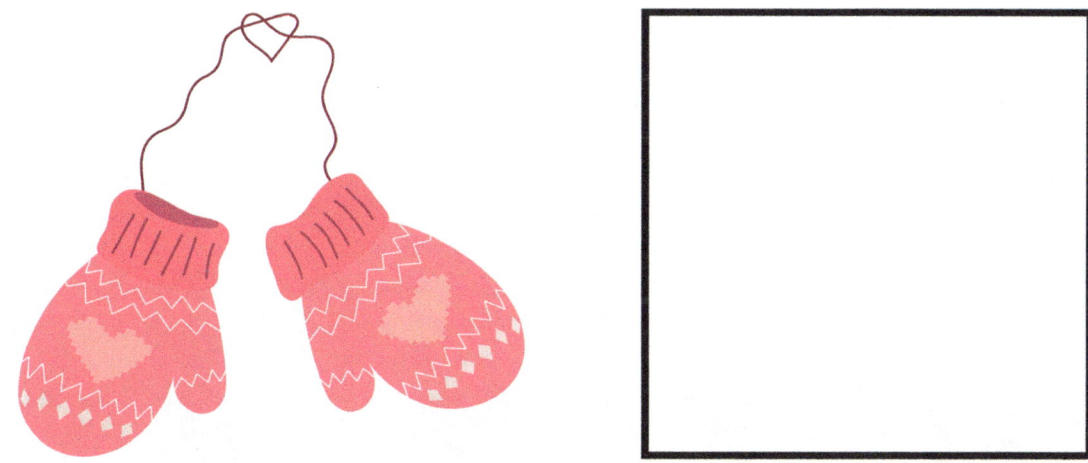

Jubilee of Jokes

What did one heart say to the other heart?
You're beating just for me!

What do you call a very small Valentine?
A valen-tiny!

What did the stamp say to the Valentine card?
I'm stuck on you!

Why did the skeleton break up with his Valentine?
He didn't have the guts to tell her he loved her!

What did one bee say to the other bee?
Bee mine!

What kind of candy do you give to a cat on Valentine's Day?
Kit-Kat bars!

What do you call a Valentine's Day gift that's very late?

Choco-late!

What did the heart-shaped cookie say to the frosting?

You complete me!

Why do skunks celebrate Valentine's Day?

Because they're scent-imental!

What did one volcano say to the other?
I lava you!

What did one pickle say to the other on Valentine's Day?
You mean a great dill to me!

What do you call a snowman's Valentine?
Love at frost sight!

What do you call two birds in love?
Tweethearts!

What do ghosts say to each other on Valentine's Day?
You're boo-tiful!

What did the boy drum say to the girl drum on Valentine's Day?
My heart beats for you!

Why didn't the skeleton send any Valentine cards?
His heart wasn't in it!

What did the donut say to the jelly?
You're the filling in my heart!

What do you write in a slug's Valentine's card?
I'm sliming my way into your heart!

What do you call a love letter from a cow?

A mooo-sage of love!

Why did the tomato turn red on Valentine's Day?

It saw the salad dressing!

Why did the candle go out with its Valentine?

It found them de-light-ful!

What did the raspberry say to the blueberry on Valentine's Day?
I love you berry much!

Why did the chocolate go to the Valentine's Day party?
Because it was sweet on everyone!

What did the cucumber say to the pickle on Valentine's Day?
You are dill-iteful to me!

Cupid's Coloring Fun

HAPPY

VALENTINE'S DAY

Thank You for Joining Our Valentine's Adventure!

We hope you had a sweet time solving puzzles, counting hearts, and laughing at all the Valentine's Day jokes in **Valentine's Math Fun for Kids!** You've done an amazing job, and we're so proud of you for completing this fun and educational journey.

If you enjoyed this book, we'd love to hear from you!

Your feedback helps us create even more exciting puzzle books for learners of all ages. Please consider leaving a review on your favorite book site and sharing your experience with others—it means the world to us!

More Fun Awaits!

If you're ready for more puzzles and adventures, be sure to check out our other books. At **MFN Goods**, we offer a whole collection of themed puzzle books filled with word searches, sudoku, mazes, and more!

Whether you're looking for more holiday fun, curious about animals, or just love a good brain-teaser, we have something for everyone.

Thank you for choosing **MFN Goods** to be part of your learning journey. Keep up the great work, and remember—learning is always sweeter with creativity and imagination!

Happy Valentine's Day and happy puzzling. We hope to see you again soon! ❤️

Made in the USA
Coppell, TX
31 January 2025

45223562R00063